DOGBERRY'S LANTERN

DOGBERRY'S LANTERN

CONSTABLE OF THE WATCH
SWINGING THE OLD BLUE LAMP

Glenn Gilbertson

Matador
9 Priory Business Park,
Wistow Road, Kibworth Beauchamp,
Leicestershire. LE8 0RX
Tel: 0116 279 2299
Email: books@troubador.co.uk
Web: www.troubador.co.uk/matador
Twitter: @matadorbooks

ISBN 978 1 80046 190 1

British Library Cataloguing in Publication Data.
A catalogue record for this book is available from the British Library.

Printed and bound in the UK by TJ Books Ltd, Padstow, Cornwall
Typeset in 12pt Adobe Garamond Pro by Troubador Publishing Ltd, Leicester, UK

Matador is an imprint of Troubador Publishing Ltd

For Elspeth and Peter

Never stop asking questions

"You are thought here to be the most senseless
and fit man for the constable of the watch;
therefore bear you the lantern."
Dogberry

William Shakespeare
Much Ado About Nothing
(Act 3, Scene 3)

Contents

Contents

Foreword

Old men enjoy telling war stories but even I began to notice when the same old yarns kept coming up time and again, and it had become a challenge to make sure that the details didn't vary too much from one telling to another, especially when some of the same people might have been present last time. Mrs Dogberry had been nagging me or, as she would put it, 'suggesting', for some time that I should write down some of my tales for the enlightenment of future generations but it was not until Titania, one of the rotating editors of the village magazine, asked me to put in something for the amusement of the good people of the village that it began to come together. Initially my thought was to do half a dozen one-page contributions but two years later I was still going.

Who do I see as a reader? Well, I'd like to think that my children and grandchildren might find it interesting, if only to see that Grandad wasn't always just an old man with a vague aroma of disinfectant and broccoli but had actually been to places and done things, although the littlest Dogberrys are still very young and it's likely that I won't be available to answer their questions by the time they can read this. I hope they'll understand how sad I am about that. Otherwise, one or two people who saw the village mag articles might be interested to read them again but this time in rather longer form and a more logical kind of order.

I have never thought of myself as being other than British, not simply English, but as the years rolled up away from home, especially living and working in environments where I was the only native English-speaking, British expat I began to see my country rather more as an outsider and realised that Johnny Foreigner might actually have had a point about some of the criticisms levelled at us. Please don't interpret the previous over-extended sentence as having any kind of political significance. I really couldn't care less whether you wanted to 'Remain' or 'Leave' or live in a country ruled by an hereditary council of sinistrines. (But if you have political views and didn't vote, don't complain about the government. I am happy to declare here how I have voted in every election or referendum for which I have been eligible. I voted 'secretly' and will continue to do so.) However, in the same way that I think I can now be objective about my country, I feel that time has given me a better perspective on what youthful Dogberry was really like. Plumbing the depths of memory doesn't just mean looking down through crystal waters. More often it's like draining the canal; as the muddy waters recede the old bicycles, prams and supermarket trollies emerge and there are some pretty murky fish in there but it's still worth looking for the sparkling gems.

In order to preserve reputations and confidences I have combined many of the various events and characters into composites to illustrate the kind of things I've been involved in and the fascinating people I've met along the way. Everything here actually took place somewhere at some time but it has not been my intention to embarrass anyone so if you think you recognise yourself, and you're pleased with the description, that's good. If you don't like what I've said, obviously I was talking about someone else. I am grateful to Master Shakespeare for his help in supplying many of the aliases but, otherwise, I have not identified any individual by name except in a very few instances of people who either deserve recognition or who are so unique as to be impossible to disguise.

I

In the Beginning

1949

I'm one of that shrinking number of people who can look back from the first half of the twenty-first century to when they were born in the first half of the twentieth century. I'd like to be able to say that growing up on the outskirts of London just after the war was fun, or even use words like 'magical' but I can really only remember snapshots. I have deeply impressed memories of things which might not, in fact, have been so extraordinary but memory is a notoriously weak muscle and we invariably prefer our own version of events whether or not something actually happened that way – just speak to anyone who has ever given evidence in court. I have no basis for comparison between my life at the time and what children elsewhere may have regarded as normal. Unlike that wave of children fifteen years before me who would talk of being uprooted from cities targeted by the Luftwaffe and sent to spend idyllically happy, or terrifyingly lonely, childhood years as evacuees, I missed out on all that and simply saw what was around me as 'normal'. I can distinctly remember, or maybe not, being taken to visit aunts, uncles and cousins in distant places in London where it looked as if the bombing had only stopped that morning. We played outside and that was okay; that was normal. I've heard the same sounds coming from children playing in the dust in Kosovo and Sudan, where they learned from one-legged siblings that they mustn't cross the yellow tapes long before they could read 'Perigo Minas'. Take a look at the faces of children on TV just about anywhere that the fighting never seems to stop; what's around them is their normal.

I had a much older cousin who was sent to fight in Korea. I was too young to have to worry about national service, although I was bitterly disappointed when I was told that I wouldn't get the chance to march around with a real rifle, and just got on with going to a series of schools as the family moved. At the time our various homes seemed to be in far separated places and it was only later I discovered that they were almost all within walking distance of each other. I saw the world through the narrow windows of my home and the school classroom and the rather wider, but highly distorting, portal of single channel, black and white television as a result of which I knew, as an incontestable fact, that all children in America rode horses to school and, from Public Information Films, that beached marine mines and unexploded ordnance on London's bomb sites were never to be played with. Public Information Films were issued in black and white featuring families from somewhere like Epsom. 'Daddy' always spoke 'Received English' very fast, had a moustache and wore a tweed suit with a collar and tie for breakfast at weekends. I'll come back to some of these things later but, for now, Dogberry was just eight years old.

After something of a religious awakening by my parents, we little Dogberrys were moved to what would now be described as a 'Faith School' and would be my final school transfer. It turned out for the best as it was a good school academically and I obtained a respectable clutch of O levels including one which I took a full eighteen months ahead of my class group with a grade A pass. At school I also formed a couple of friendships which lasted over the years. Good friends are rare but of three of us who most regularly kept company and stayed in touch afterwards, sadly, I'm the only survivor.

*

We were regularly sent out into the forest on cross-country runs, unescorted, without hi-vis fluorescent vests, GPS trackers or bodyguards, over paths for which no risk assessment had been made. My friends, Leonato and Benedick, and I found that if we could dodge the pack about 200 yards from the gate, we could pick up a forest path, take a short cut to a lake and wade out to an island. There we waited while the others ran their four miles and looped back past the lake on their way back to the school allowing us to join in at the end, muddy, wet and cold and never for a moment considering how much extra effort we had put into not doing it right. Incredibly, we were never caught.

Leo was one of the first people I'd met when I joined the school and we were actually quite an unlikely pair to form a friendship. He was a very keen footballer, captain of the school team and played just about any sport or ball game with the sort of relaxed flair and skill I've never had and therefore usually found intensely annoying. However, we both had quite serious academic aspirations and shared most classes through until we left school in 1965. Towards the end of the last term it was usual for more and more free periods to appear in the timetable as public examinations in various subjects were taken until, in the last couple of weeks, we were both almost completely unencumbered by any kind of academic distractions and struggled to fill our time. As Leo had been elevated to head boy that year, and I was one of the first prefects to have been appointed, we thus didn't even have the usual constraints placed on most other pupils and could roam virtually at will enjoying the complete, but misplaced, confidence of the staff.

*

Don't Try This at Home

The Devil finds work for idle hands and ours were about as idle as it was possible to be without actually being in a coma. I can't remember who started the conversation but we had been talking about the problems of drilling through glass. Please don't ask why; it was a pointless conversation and led to an experiment in an empty workshop over a lunchtime but let's be charitable and call it research. The first test piece was a thick-bottomed tumbler borrowed from the dining hall. Surprise – it broke but, undaunted, we tried again and found that it was possible to get a small hole through about once in four tries. Of course, that meant a failure rate of seventy-five per cent but still quite impressive. We managed to collect four or five self-draining tumblers during about a week of trying which we then mixed in with others in the dining hall and sat back quietly smirking as they turned up one by one at lunchtime; even a nun on the staff got one – double points for that. Again, never tumbled, although strongly suspected by the deputy head before we left the school three days later. *Quis custodiet ipsos custodes.*

And Certainly Don't Try This at School

If I am remembered at the school at all, however, it will not be for academic distinction or sporting prowess but for breaking two of the headmaster's ribs in a game of beach rugby during a school trip to Italy. That was certainly a first at the time and I doubt it has been equalled since. The headmaster was an ancient forty-one-year-old who'd played rugby at university. Our teachers obviously thought that they were able to handle an informal game against a group of unpractised fifteen-year-olds but forgot that a lack of experience often equates to an absence of fear. I will always remember the snapping sound, like a dry twig, as my shoulder went into the side of the gentleman's chest and the wheezing noise he made trying to suck in his next breath. Of course, it was an accident but my penance was to be available as an arm to lean on for the rest of the trip.

A propensity for causing serious injuries to teachers does, however, seem to have been inherited by my daughter, Desdemona, who managed to get a javelin through the upper thigh of her school's games/ phys. ed. teacher. Worse still, the poor lady was mentoring a student teacher at the time on the safe management of a school sports day. "Come on, Desdemona, throw it. Don't worry, you'll never get it this fa…" My daughter claims that if you measure from where she threw it to where it touched down in the hospital accident and emergency department over six miles away it must still stand as a world record.

*

Leonato, aka Andy Vale, was probably the closest friend I had in school and afterwards. When we all marched off to become taxpayers in 1965, Andy went into the offices of Canadian Pacific, the international shipping company, at their UK head office in Trafalgar Square. Over the years he became a specialist expert in transport and logistics and developed their in-house transport company in Tilbury. At various times he ran operations in Antwerp and, for several months, worked on a logistics project in California. Most of us have pocketed the odd pencil or a couple of paper clips from the office but Andy, always one to do things in style, went one better and in 1969, when Julie came to work at the same company, he married her. I was privileged to be the best man at their wedding although I'm not sure I've ever told her how near they came to not getting married that day when we found some of the papers needed by the priest had not arrived. She had enough on her mind so it's probably best she didn't know. Andy retired in 2003 and spent the next few years happily enjoying life with Julie, their children and grandchildren. In October 2010 Andy collapsed at their home in Essex. His brain tumour was inoperable and he died in February 2011 with Julie and his family beside him. Much missed.

1965

As my years of educational internment crawled towards conclusion, I'd started to become vaguely aware that I would have to get involved in the tedious business of earning a living sooner or later. The most obvious choice would have been some kind of industrial apprenticeship, of which lots were then available as the country still made things in various metal bashing factories and a 'Made in Britain' label meant quality, reliability and value. I flirted briefly with the notion of going into law and becoming a solicitor, and even picked up a couple of the A levels necessary to start, but the idea of another five years of study to become an articled clerk at Snatch, Grabbit & Runne was too daunting. Thankfully, however, I was nudged gently away from either course by a headmaster (he of the broken ribs but more about him later) who suggested teaching as a serious option. That was strongly supported by my mother but my brother, Balthazar, a couple of years older, had joined the City of London Police and was clearly enjoying such an exciting life that I applied for the Metropolitan Police – the Met. I was three inches shorter than Balthazar and couldn't have got in even if I had applied for the City. My life was now locked onto the course it would follow for the next thirty-odd years but, first, I was going to spend a couple of years as a cadet where a mixture of military-style basic training (all our instructors were ex-army), preparatory police training and camping in wild, cold and wet parts of Britain would be enjoyed at the expense of the British taxpayer. To those of you who were taxpayers during those years, my sincere thanks; I think you invested wisely.

Joining the Metropolitan Police Cadet Corps meant that sixteen-year-old Dogberry left home, not just for the week but, effectively, for good and I never lived with my parents and family again. I was enrolled in the Cadet Corp Training School at Hendon where the lifestyle and system of organisation were somewhere between being in the army, a good public school and a Victorian prison. New recruits slept in very large barrack huts which allowed about four square yards of floor space in which all personal equipment and private property had to be stored. (Bed metal grey demountable x1; mattress x1; locker metal grey (short) x1; locker metal grey (long) x1; blankets green x3; sheets white x2; pillow x1; pillowcase white x1; floor-mat grey 18"x24" x1.)

There were twenty-eight of us in my first home-from-home and we had to make sure it was kept in gleaming condition to be ready for the weekly inspection and frequent, unannounced, supervisory visits. The day started with a siren at 06.30 after which there could be a session on the assault course, training in the gym, drill (we did a lot of that), or classroom lessons on police administration systems, powers, procedures and law. Entries in a pocket report book still had to be made in pencil and not ink. It was not until 1968, after I had become a constable in training school, that the senior command levels of the Metropolitan Police were persuaded that ball-pen technology was sufficiently reliable that Laszlo Biro's invention could be used despite having been produced commercially since about 1895 and in common use for the last thirty-odd years.

A local college provided lecturers on a range of subjects such as history, mathematics, literature and constitutional law leading to higher-level public examinations. Overall, we spent about thirty-five per cent of the day on police specific training, another thirty-five per cent on fitness and physical development, thirty-five per cent on non-police related academic studies, twenty-five per cent drilling under an ex-Guards RSM, and fifteen per cent on kit cleaning and maintenance. Yes, I can add up; we were kept very busy. The rest of the day was free but it was expected that everyone would sign up for some kind of extra-curricular activity. As a result, I learned to touch-type and discovered a skill with a rifle that I had never suspected. Cadets were responsible for security and were assigned to evening and weekend patrol duties around the training school about every six weeks. Leave was taken according to the academic year but camping trips, training for treks across Dartmoor in search of the legendary Ten Tors or canoeing up endless waterways were fitted into these periods of downtime.

The Cadet Corps was my first real introduction to people of my own age from elsewhere in the realm or outside what would now be termed my socio-economic/demographic group. I was aware that people outside London spoke strangely, TV had taught me that much, but it was disorientating to have the only London accent in a squad of thirty of my peers. When an ex-Scots Guards drill instructor, whose Glaswegian accent needed sub-titles, bellowed "Cockney – one pace forward" (or "*Kawkni – win pis f'wid*") it was only the helpful interpreter beside me in the rank hissing from the side of his mouth "*Dawgbry. Ees tawkin tey yooo*" who enabled me to comply as briskly as was required.

*

The first black police officer in the UK was John Kent, the British-born son of a former Caribbean slave, who served in Carlisle in 1837. In 1967, the Met recruited its very first black constable, indeed the first in the UK for over a hundred years and the first non-white female police officer arrived in 1968. The Cadet Corps was still very much an all-male environment where membership was certainly not as socially representative or ethnically mixed as it might have been but changes in perceptions and attitudes were beginning which would spread into the wider Met during my career. Did they come about as fast as they should have done? Certainly not, but society generally was also slow to react. Credit for spurring on those changes in attitudes undoubtedly goes principally to the news media, various pressure groups and individuals, some of whom were extremely vociferous and overtly hostile, who looked at policing from the outside but I don't think the contribution from within the police service itself has been properly acknowledged. Whatever the reasons, change did happen and is still happening; a good thing, too.

*

Much of our training aimed to develop fitness, confidence and leadership, so we spent a lot of time climbing hills and dangling from ropes in Wales or doing cross-country runs in Kent carrying heavy twelve-foot-long wooden poles between three of us, actually much more difficult than with just two as everyone must keep perfectly in step. I have crossed innumerable bottomless chasms using just a dozen lengths of cord and the same ubiquitously useful wooden poles. I understood the contribution this might make to 'fitness' and 'confidence' but it was only years later, at the staff college at Bramshill, when I was invited to take part in a similar chasm-crossing exercise and said, "You do it. Let me know how you get on" that the leadership penny dropped. Good managers can do whatever needs doing but good leaders get people to do things for them. I still enjoy visiting north Wales and would love to be able to go climbing there again but, sadly, that's not going to happen.

There is no Statute of Limitations in British law so I have no intention of telling you, even now, when or where the following events took place nor the identities of those involved. Suffice to say that everyone concerned, I think with two exceptions, has since gone to sing with the Choir Invisible.

Many years ago and far, far away, teams of four cadets were sent out on an exercise in an area which might have looked a lot like north Wales. They had no money but had been provided with tents, kit, food and two map grid references showing where to camp overnight so that the supervising staff, two sergeant instructors in an old Land Rover, could periodically check that they were still alive. This was described as an *escape and evasion* exercise (you'll remember I said that the training was very 'military'), and between campsites they would lose points for being seen on the move but earn extra credit for initiative and, of course, being first back in three days.

On the first night they found that the campsite grid reference was one digit out leaving them to solve the problem of pitching tents on a steep and heavily wooded slope. The instructors visited about two hours after sunset when they grudgingly conceded that their trainees' map reading was perfect but they should still have used their initiative and a bit of 'common f*****g sense' to pick a better campsite. Day two passed without further problem but on day three, still twenty miles from the finish line, hungry, tired and foot-sore, they tramped into a village where one of them knew the landlady of the pub – she was the mother of his girlfriend and only too pleased to see them. Four steak pies and beers later the world seemed like a much nicer place until they heard the highly distinctive rattle of a diesel-engine Land Rover 88 coming into the car park. The two instructors entered the bar just a moment too late to see four cadets dive over the counter to hide, if not actually under, then very close to the skirts of the landlady. She took the new customers' orders for lunch and kept them engaged in conversation about the weather for as long as she could before preparing their food with meticulous, slow, care. Had her latest two patrons looked outside they might have seen their vehicle (no steering-locks in those days and vehicle security was rudimentary at best) being free-wheeled out of the car park and bump-started further down the hill. An hour later they realised their predicament but, as they shouldn't have been in the pub in the first place, they decided to get to the finish line by taxi while pondering what to do next.

Meanwhile, their Land Rover made its way to a point about a couple of miles from the finish where it was abandoned and later recovered by two very relieved instructors. The trainees were careful not to be the first team home – that honour went to four colleagues who had improperly hitched a ride on a farm tractor. They still got good marks for their overall orienteering skill but spent the next couple of months worried that they might be identified as the Land Rover thieves, not knowing that their instructors were equally profoundly anxious about their own failure to report the misappropriation of an official vehicle. Nothing happened and the incident drifted back into the mists of memory.

Years later, during a wet, cold night duty, a uniformed sergeant, no longer an instructor, was trying to convince himself that the tepid brown fluid in his mug was indeed coffee and chatting with a newly promoted inspector who had once been a cadet under his charge. The Mysterious Case of the Disappearing Land Rover came up and the sergeant choked on his drink as wisdom lit up his face and he spluttered, "So, it was you! It was you... Sir."

*

Not everything we did was slanted towards vehicle theft and fitness and I recall with great pleasure assisting with a six-month course for half a dozen very severely disabled children in their school's physiotherapy pool. Their ages ranged from about twelve to sixteen and they could do almost nothing for themselves but had sparkling personalities. Two helpers per child were needed in the water with them plus the qualified physiotherapist who supervised the session. It was physically demanding work and involved supporting and exercising the kids in water which felt hot enough to make tea. I hadn't realised it was possible to work up a sweat in a swimming pool. I found out later that they probably had a life expectancy of about twenty to thirty years; they had significant physical limitations but were intelligent, sharp and engaging. The older ones almost certainly knew what the future looked like. I hope we helped to make what time they had a little more enjoyable.

*

At eighteen I had completed all the necessary training and academic courses required and the last few months of my time as a Met cadet were spent on attachment to a London police station, patrolling and working regular early/late/night duty shifts for the first time. Somewhat fitter and, in those days, slimmer than the average PC, there was a tendency to be used as a gofer on any task that needed more than moderate exertion. If I was assigned to patrol with the station van on night duty, I knew it was probably because they still hadn't got round to replacing the battery and I'd have to push-start it whenever there wasn't a convenient slope.

We were called to a nineteenth-century block of flats one night because an elderly man who lived there hadn't been seen for several days. The front door had been very well reinforced and wasn't going to yield to anything less than ten minutes with a very large axe. "That's okay," said my supervising PC, "I'll send the lad up the drainpipe and he can get in through the kitchen window." That sort of skipped over the fact that it was a second-floor flat and I hadn't yet done the burglary drainpipe-climbing course but cadets were cheap and expendable. It was a good, solid and secure iron drainpipe which ran directly beside the kitchen windows all the way from the top floor and turned out to be a remarkably easy climb, something to be noted as a point for home security. I made enough noise to attract a sizeable audience from other kitchen windows on the way up and was very happy to find the second-floor window partly open. The window itself was small but I squeezed through and fumbled around in the dark having left my torch in my overcoat down below. In the living room the TV was switched on and turned up quite loud which was why my entry hadn't been noticed by the elderly couple watching it. Uniformed figures climbing in through the back of their flat were apparently unremarkable enough not to cause any alarm whatsoever and the lady was even kind enough to offer to make me a cup of tea before letting me climb out of her kitchen window again to get into the flat next door, where I found the occupant lying peacefully, dead and very cold, on his bedroom floor. No violence, no disturbance, nothing missing, no burglary gone wrong; he'd just quietly and alone run out of the allocation of heartbeats which had lasted him from 1880 to 1967. RIP.

Over the years Met cadets have spread out from Hendon to become police officers in every constabulary in the UK and many elsewhere around the world; a significant number achieved middle rank and a few the most senior command levels. Some have become published authors on an eclectic range of subjects, athletes to represent their county at national level or country at international level. Some have gone into politics. Two of my personal friends were killed on duty and, I'm sure, others I did not know myself. At least one, and probably others, ended up in prison.

II

If You Can't Take a Joke...

1968

Eventually the Met decided that it had invested quite enough resources in preparing me to police the capital and I joined training school – 'Peel House' in Westminster, not Hendon. I now held the office of constable, a status conferred under oath by a Justice of the Peace and granting power by law to make arrests in circumstances that members of the public could not; I could conduct searches of the person without the consent of the person searched and I was absolutely terrified. Of the three best pieces of advice I've ever been given, the second-best was "Learn to talk to people but never let them see the fear in your eyes". Then "You'll slide further on bullshit than you will on gravel". But the most valuable, by far, was "If you can't take a joke you shouldn't have joined".

Military officers derive their authority from their commission, letters of appointment signed by the sovereign. Police do not have a 'commission' but are given the powers in law of the 'office of constable' by a warrant, an order signed by a Justice of the Peace. They are therefore correctly called 'officers' regardless of rank which causes endless fun dealing with military personnel in the UK and with police elsewhere in the world where they usually adhere to the military model.

Life as a recruit in the training school wasn't markedly different from what I had experienced for the last three years as a cadet. My cadet corps background meant I was rather more used to the Met's style of discipline but otherwise did not confer any significant advantage over other members of my class who had joined after careers in industry, commerce or service in the armed forces. Indeed, it was slightly disadvantageous to be the youngest recruit, maybe by ten years. However, much of the curriculum was familiar and after thirteen weeks of basic training I passed out of the gates to begin my first assignment. I was despatched to M Division HQ at Southwark Police Station, where I was issued with some new toys which would be with me for many years, namely my truncheon, whistle and chain, police-box key and duty band. I was then forwarded, like a parcel, to Carter Street Police Station where I would spend the next four years.

*

If you have a rummage down the back of the sofa, or through the wife's drawers in the kitchen, you may well come across an old police whistle. You will often see them for sale on bric-a-brac stalls in markets and antique shops where the price will depend on the dealer's sense of humour. Prior to the introduction of whistles, and when radios would have been regarded as akin to magic, police in the street communicated by shouting or with wooden football rattles. Apart from being very heavy and cumbersome these were also not really very effective. In 1884 a representative of whistle-makers J Hudson and Company, later to become Acme Whistles, demonstrated his company's products on Clapham Common and proved they could be heard a mile away. Small, with no moving parts (don't confuse it with the referee's snail whistle containing a large wooden ball), it was policeman-proof and cheaper than a rattle. The company was awarded a contract to supply 10,000 and further contracts followed.

Eventually they would be making whistles for every police force in the country and many elsewhere in the world. Soldiers in the trenches heard these whistles to urge them to go over the top – often the very last thing they heard.

Take a closer look at yours next time because there are still some gems like mine out there waiting to be found. If it has the name 'J Hudson & Company' on the barrel it could be an original. It might also be engraved with the name of the police force for which it was made. The early ones were 'Metropolitan Police', but the real clue to its age is the company address. J Hudson & Co. operated from 84 Buckingham Street, Birmingham from 1883 to 1884 then in 1885 they moved to 131 Barr Street where they stayed until 1888. (Please bear with me if this is a bit detailed but you'll thank me later when you pay a pound for something worth fifty.) In 1888 they moved to 13 Barr Street where they remained until 1909. In 1909 the company moved to 244 Barr Street where they still make whistles including the classic 'Acme' snail whistles loved by referees and traffic policemen the world over. All these addresses are within walking distance of each other. Mine bears the maker's name, a serial number and the address at 84 Buckingham Street which the company have confirmed means it was part of the original contract to supply the Met. It was already eighty-five years old when it was issued to me and has been in my possession for over fifty years. Allowing for periods sitting on a shelf in police station storerooms I would guess that no more than four or five other officers have carried it over the years. It would be fascinating to trace the histories of those to whom it was issued and where it had been since it was made, but issue of 'appointments', including the whistle, duty band and truncheon were recorded by the divisional storeman in handwritten ledgers which, sadly, no longer exist. It could have been present during Queen Victoria's Jubilee celebrations, 'Votes for Women' marches and disturbances stirred up by Sir Oswald Mosley. Certainly, it would have been used during air raids in the war years and lining the route to the palace for the Coronation in 1953. By the time of Winston Churchill's funeral in

1965 it was probably back in the stores awaiting reissue but it was on the street again with me in Grosvenor Square outside the US Embassy in 1968 during demonstrations against the war in Vietnam. In all the time I carried it I never once had the opportunity to use it. What's it worth? At over 135 years old – priceless.

*

The whistle came with a chain and a key to open police boxes which were introduced in the early twentieth century. My key might even itself be over a hundred years old and one of the very first to be issued. It could have been on the same chain with the whistle for a very long time and likewise it would have passed through several pairs of hands. Apart from police boxes the key also opened 'posts' (small telephone boxes at the roadside or bolted to a convenient lamp post) as well as the front door of every police station in London; we were not very good at security in those days. The other keys on my chain were an old handcuff key and my locker key. About fifteen years after leaving the station I happened to visit and looked in the locker room out of curiosity. Amazingly, my locker was still there with my name and number on the door. It wasn't the time capsule I was hoping for and held only an old pair of black boots, now an amusing shade of green, a report of a minor road accident which the process section had sent back to me for correction in 1971 and enough spiders for a BBC2 nature programme.

Next came the duty band which was a vertically striped blue and white armlet about two inches wide that went around the left sleeve a couple of inches above the cuff. They were introduced in the very early days of policing because constables and sergeants, like soldiers, wore their uniforms on and off duty and the striped band indicated when the wearer was 'on' duty. Originally the stripes ran around the sleeve rather like a naval officer's rank 'rings' but that was later changed; I don't know when or why, certainly before my time. There was even a specific disciplinary offence of removing a duty band with 'intent to deceive' a public house licensee in order to purchase 'or acquire' alcoholic drink (it came up in my promotion exam). Outside of London I can't find a record of any other police force that used duty bands but there might have been some in the nineteenth century. I wore mine in the Met until 1971 when I had to hang up my uniform to become a temporary detective constable. The Met discontinued use of them shortly afterwards and now only the City of London Police still wear them, but with red and white stripes, on the dress uniform of constables and sergeants.

Oh yes, the truncheon. This absolutely useless lump of wood was carried in a concealed trouser pocket twenty inches long while the truncheon, always called a 'stick', was sixteen inches long. Drivers and CID officers were issued with an even shorter ten-inch version. It got in the way if you had to move quickly and getting it out to use it, from under a tunic and greatcoat, was not easy so it was usually simpler just to leave it in a locker at the station. Some of the older ones were made of heavy black 'iron wood' but mine was lighter and made of a red wood similar to mahogany. It's basically a club, or cudgel, and as a defensive weapon is from a technology unchanged since Og picked up a broken tree branch outside his cave to whack Ug over the head. I still have it and, like my whistle, it's never been used.

*

In November 1963, the BBC set out quite deliberately to terrify future generations of children by exposing them to foam rubber special-effects monsters, sci-fi storylines without any basis whatever in actual science, and an electronic theme tune which most of us would be able to hum even now without having to think about it. *Doctor Who* (no first name and suspiciously vague about the academic discipline in which he had been awarded his doctorate), wandered impossibly through the universe in his TARDIS, 'Time And Relative Dimension In Space', machine, a confusing contraption with seemingly unlimited power resources and an infinitely large interior yet strangely restricted in relation to its exterior dimensions. Although the doctor had a profound knowledge of all things scientific he seemed unable to repair an important mechanism of his Tardis which should have allowed it to automatically blend, chameleon-like, with its environment of the moment. Even at fourteen, I was never quite able to accept Dad's explanation that the 'Tardis was out of warranty. It was a time-machine after all! Why not just run it back to the factory to a time when the warranty was still valid? I also knew that serious machines came with owner's handbooks and workshop manuals – about this time I had myself changed a defective starter motor on Dad's car with just the handbook to guide me. How difficult could a Tardis be to someone of the doctor's skill? But in almost sixty years he has been unable to find the owner's handbook and the defect has never been rectified.

The fault had obviously only just developed in 1963 as the chosen outward appearance was that of a police box. No doubt this was selected initially because someone in programme development thought that yet another police box would go unnoticed on the streets of London while the props department either had an old one in stock or had only to knock up a convincing looking replica to solve their scenery problems for a very long time to come. In truth it was more likely that a London police box could have magically appeared in eighteenth-century revolutionary France without the twitch of a Gallic eyebrow, than to have materialised on a street corner in London where it would immediately have drawn hostile attention. Local residents looking for somewhere to deposit used fish and chip wrappers, dead cats or even call police, would quickly have realised that something odd was happening. The greatest threat, however, would be from local police officers who would want to know who had planted a new box on their beat. Every officer in London had a key which opened **every** police box and it's strange to think that I could have stumbled into the Tardis by mistake. It would appear that the average Time Lord wasn't as mechanically competent as he would have us think and understood nothing about home security.

*

You will probably have guessed by now that my intention is to talk about police boxes and leave BBC sci-fi to anorak-wearers. Police boxes first appeared in London in the early twentieth century as an idea borrowed from the USA where they had already been in use for many years. I don't have to describe one – you've all seen *Doctor Who* – but I can assure you that the interior dimensions were a lot less generous than the BBC spec. Made of concrete and painted inside in a sickly, tobacco-stained white, the only furnishings were a fitted desk and a tall wooden stool, if it hadn't been reassigned to more important duties as the umpire's chair in the station snooker room. A small shelf contained a set of maps of the local division's beats and patrols, an *A to Z London* (1932 edition with half the index missing) and, most importantly, the box ring book. There was also a small cabinet containing a telephone, accessible also to the public from outside, which gave direct contact to the police station switchboard – and not to Scotland Yard as most members of the public believed. The telephone had no bell but an incoming call flashed a light on the roof of the box.

Today every police officer carries a personal radio providing instant communication and location but when police boxes first appeared, even the electric telephone was cutting-edge technology. By 1963, when *Doctor Who* landed, or 1968, when PC Dogberry landed, telephones were still the standard means of communication but radios were beginning to appear. The area covered from Carter Street Police Station, just off the Walworth Road, extended from Elephant & Castle to Denmark Hill and from Kennington Park to Peckham. Without transport it might take more than an hour to reach some of the more remote parts. When I was posted to the station, it had just four Storno personal radios. These were issued to the duty officer, rarely leaving the station, the section sergeant, rarely leaving the charge room, the van driver, rarely leaving the canteen, and the area car, rarely leaving the drivers' locker. Communication on urgent matters was made by teleprinter from Scotland Yard to the station and VHF radio to the vehicles. Foot patrol officers, not allowed to sit in a police vehicle until they had at least three years' service, had to maintain contact by meeting the section sergeant at predetermined times and places or by making a 'ring', a scheduled call, to the station. Routine messages could then be passed and the duty officer could be assured that all of his officers had been accounted for.

Old Kent Road runs from Tower Bridge Road to Peckham and was the border between Carter Street and Tower Bridge divisions. Too far from the station to justify the forty-five-minute walk back to the station just to check in, officers on Old Kent Road patrol and the adjoining beats instead went to 11 Box opposite the corner of Old Kent Road and Albany Road to call Carter Street's switchboard. Technically this was on the neighbouring division but patrolling constables were graciously permitted to cross the road for this purpose. The desk provided somewhere to write up reports of accidents and take refreshments and, on a cold night, it was not uncommon to find four or five officers squeezed into an area about four feet by four feet (before metrication). Smoking was then obligatory and the atmosphere inside often made it difficult to see who was actually there. Having made a ring, the fact and time were duly entered in the box 'ring book' and patrol resumed. Missing a ring was a crime against GOD (Good Order and Discipline). Three minutes late would bring a very stern rebuke from the section sergeant. Ten minutes late was ten times worse and would certainly incur the displeasure of colleagues who had been called away from card games or snooker to assist a search. Dragging the van driver away from his game of pontoon to look for a missing probationer was a serious matter – the little sod had better be seriously injured or he'd be buying teas for the van and area car crews for the rest of his career. Being missing for half an hour could only be justified by death or having made an arrest.

*

Just being close to a box affected people in strange ways. I once worked with a colleague who had the conversational sparkle of a Dalek on a Monday morning when making a ring but I think that probably had more to do with Newcastle Brown Ale than a desire to 'exterminate' and conquer the universe (although some of us were in doubt at times). Whatever the reason he would always have a report to write up necessitating long spells in the box. The public, however, have a quite amazing capacity for self-delusion and flatly refuse to accept what is clearly true, preferring, like many jurors, even the most outlandish alternative theory. A lady in Bermondsey was convinced that police boxes gave access to a system of secret underground police tunnels able to transport officers almost instantaneously from place to place. She knew this was so because she had once used the telephone to call for help and a constable in uniform had almost immediately stepped out of the door. How else could this have been possible?

It was fashionable in the 1960s for students, accepted as being the most stupid people on the planet, to compete to see how many could be shoe-horned into a Mini – 'car' that is, not 'skirt'. The prize was fifteen-minutes' fame and an interview with someone like Simon Dee or some other national TV notable. I'm not sure what the record was but it was into double figures. The Met police equivalent challenge was to jam an entire relief into a police box. I've seen seven PCs emerge from one box and while this may not have been a Met record it was almost certainly a divisional best. My most memorable experience was seeing the look on the face of a small boy of about six, just learning his first four-letter expletives, who looked at me wide-eyed as I stepped out of 11 Box. "No", he said, he hadn't seen any Daleks so far that day but promised to let me know if he did. As personal radios became more common, even to the point of having one each, and police transport was issued more widely, the role of the police box diminished. An evening came in late 1971 when I made my way along the Old Kent Road, fish and chips still warm under my raincoat, only to find a square of concrete on the pavement where 11 Box had been – seems I had missed the memo and another little bit of police culture had slipped unnoticed into history.

III

On the Road

The Case of the Naked Lady

In the 1950s the Metropolitan Police realised that travelling from place to place on foot was probably not going to work for much longer. Foot patrols, the traditional but highly ineffective 'bobby-on-the-beat', so dear to politicians looking for votes and newspapers trying to stop those same politicians from being elected, still had a place, indeed still have a place, but really only as a visible presence to reassure the public that they're getting some sort of value for money from their local authority police precept. In fact, foot patrols didn't do very much at all unless it was possible to flood an area with so many bobbies-on-the-beat that they tripped over each other. Of course, any police officer with more than about ten years' experience would be able to relate numerous incidents when he (always 'he' then – the ladies were far too intelligent to get involved with policing on foot in the rain) was able to bring some major felon to book with a bold example of singular policing skill and courage. With a few notable exceptions most of these stories involved another officer or, like fine wines, greatly improved with age.

Motor cars were still very expensive and for urban patrolling and carrying despatches, what was needed was a small, easy to ride, preferably silent, motorcycle. (Trumpet fanfare, roll of drums and…) Enter the Velocette LE (Little Engine) Lightweight Patrol Motorcycle manufactured by Veloce Ltd, in Hall Green, Birmingham which, in London, became known almost immediately as the 'Noddy' bike. This had nothing to do with Noddy, an elf-like child known for driving a yellow and red car underage and living in a questionable relationship with an overweight bearded elf called Big Ears. The name apparently arose because (Metropolitan) police regulations required constables and sergeants, if properly dressed in uniform, including headgear, to snap a formal salute to any officer in uniform (including headgear) of the rank of inspector or above. Someone at the time must have thought that it was not a good idea to take your right hand off the controls to salute the duty officer and riders were instead allowed to offer a courteous nod of the head – Noddy bikes were 'go'. Traffic patrol riders, who could roll and smoke a cigarette while driving a 650cc Triumph Saint, were Knights of the Road and did not acknowledge the existence of mere uniformed 'officers', much less salute them.

*

I will now admit to a void in my life. I have never owned or ridden a motorcycle – but I've always wanted to. In 1970, having just completed my two-year probationary period, I was offered the chance to go to the police driving school at Hendon. In police driving terms this was the equivalent of a pilot being offered a jet-fighter flying course but I thought about it for maybe a microsecond before I accepted. However, there was a catch. My divisional superintendent, not God but probably on first name terms with Him, had decided to place the division's three Noddy bikes under control of the enquiries section where the riders would do nothing but report road accidents and traffic offences. I wanted to go into the CID and the Noddy course went instead to a colleague on the relief. I was not envious. Yes, I was – very.

Had I gone on to do that course I would have been instructed in such essential policing skills as driving while sitting on the handlebars facing backwards and standing on the saddle with an arm outstretched like a self-propelled statue of Lenin hailing the Future of Socialism. A constable at Hammersmith, where I was a cadet, only ever rode this way on night duty. Several times I explained to incredulous observers that this was an official technique to allow the rider an elevated viewing platform to prevent and detect crime. Tourists can usually be induced to believe most things if presented without a smile. "Trust me. I'm a policeman."

The Velocette, while very quiet, was not silent and the water-cooled engine made a very distinctive sound; nothing sounded like a Noddy except another Noddy – ask any anorakista with ten enamel badges. In London, just about all Velocettes were Noddy bikes and probably alerted far more burglars than they ever contributed to arresting. But the main purpose of the patrolling Noddy was not to arrest criminals, nor carry despatches. Much more importantly they collected the morning newspapers, carried two dozen bacon bagels in each pannier box and warned foot-duty colleagues sheltering in a police box that the section sergeant was coming down the road.

Every Met police officer from about 1950 to the early 1970s has a story about Noddys. Often these are the same ones with only the names and locations changed; some are even true. There was the legendary mechanic, whose workshop was known only to certain loyal Noddy riders who were sworn to secrecy. The clunky shaft drive, Velocette LE, with its hand gear change and 48mph top speed, was not designed to be fearsomely fast. But the Noddy Magician could, if you crossed his palm with a cheese and pickle sandwich, tweak this, trim that and adjust the other to enable the bolder rider to experience life at over 65mph. One of his disciples was, no doubt, the rider of the mythical Phantom Noddy reputed to cross the Met in the early hours of moonless nights. Chased, but never caught, by hunting packs of traffic patrol sergeants, all of them Class 1 advanced drivers riding the most powerful motorcycles on the fleet, the Phantom was alleged to achieve over 100mph. Well, they would say that, wouldn't they?

*

Carter Street Division in Walworth, part of the London Borough of Southwark, was chosen as the ideal location to build the Aylesbury Estate, a development of high-rise residential blocks with walkways and shops at second-floor level and interconnecting bridges which would eventually be home to over 8,000 people. The largest block, Wendover, was about half a mile long. I'm sure the model proudly unveiled by the architects at the public presentation probably looked futuristically fantastic but was rather more Fritz Lang's 'Metropolis' than urban inner London. From a policing point of view, it was a nightmare. Even before it was complete thieves would steal anything not actually welded down knowing that a police officer on another walkway would have to travel about two miles to reach them. A Noddy rider, who I'll call Claudio, was up to the challenge, however, and his silhouette could frequently be seen patrolling the rooftops of the unfinished buildings with significant success.

Claudio and his Noddy also featured in the Case of the Naked Lady on a night-duty shift around the Elephant & Castle. For those unfamiliar with the area, the Elephant & Castle was a complex road system swirling around two very large roundabouts. It replaced an infamously nightmarish series of intersections and included a labyrinthine rabbit warren of pedestrian tunnels, paths and bridges through which Claudio would roam, lights out on his (almost) silent Noddy in the early hours of the morning. The 'Elephant' was also where three police divisions met and, being the junction of four major roads, was visited frequently by police. On a very quiet night therefore, a call to a naked woman running around and through the Elephant created a perfect storm to draw in most police vehicles south of the Thames. That night I was a passenger on Mike Sierra 2, a wheezing, slow, heavy, Austin LD van usually called a 'Black Moriah' and we probably arrived on the scene last even after travelling the length of Camberwell New Road at a heady 45mph because, if an arrest was made, we would be needed to transport the prisoner.

For more than thirty minutes we searched every street, alley, footpath, overpass and tunnel not knowing if we were looking for a mentally ill lady, a simple drunk, an exhibitionist or, worst case, a victim of serious crime. No sign; no discarded clothing, no abandoned vehicles, no broken windows; nothing at all. What we did get, however, were several further similar calls from members of the public who had seen our birthday-suited quarry. We regrouped by a row of bus stops outside the London Tabernacle to discuss our next moves. An inspector even attended to take charge – and received a courteous nod from Claudio.

The inspector decided that ninety-five per cent of the Met's south London fleet was not a sensible use of police resources and sent everyone back to their assigned duties except Claudio, to carry on his search of the underworld, the van driver and me. But things now moved very fast indeed. As we broke to move back to our vehicles there was a chilling scream, the more alarming because we couldn't see immediately from whence it came but an instant later Claudio gave a choking squawk and we turned to see him sinking to his knees under the weight of a very large lady, certainly heavier than Claudio himself, who had landed astride his back from the roof of the bus shelter where she had been hiding and listening to our planning. With her arms around his neck and legs clamped around his waist, Claudio used what air remained in his lungs to ask "I say, chaps! Would you please assist this lady?" Those might not have been his exact words but that was the gist. Unfortunately, what with our uncontrollable laughter and simple caution at getting too close to the muscular and agile lady now gripping Claudio in a very professional looking strangle hold, it took a while to detach her, unharmed, and release Claudio, uninjured but very grumpy. With a cell blanket to preserve her modesty, our Venus was conveyed to the station where the duty officer broke all records to 'deem' her under the Mental Health Act and pass the whole problem over to the Maudsley Hospital at Denmark Hill.

By the late 1960s the Met had introduced Panda cars and even people like me were allowed to drive. In 1971 Veloce Ltd went into liquidation and stopped production. Kent Constabulary bought up the remaining spares to keep their own fleet on the road until 1974 but in London, within a couple of years, the Noddy was no more. The world would never be the same again.

*

Incidentally, why a police van should be called a 'Black Moriah' is not easy to settle and the name has a long and much debated history. It certainly goes back to the early nineteenth century and may have begun as a sarcastic allusion to Black Maria, a famous race horse of the period, and how long it would take a horse-drawn police van to arrive to take away a prisoner. I've not found any reference earlier than the nineteenth century but that's hardly surprising as organised official 'policing' only really started in the early 1800s. Another, probably equally credible version cited in *Brewer's Dictionary of Phrase and Fable*, suggests a respectful reference to a large and much feared lady of colour called Maria Lee. Maria, or Mariah or Moriah, reputedly ran a boarding house for sailors and would be called to help police deal with difficult or violent prisoners. Most police vans, until very recently in the UK and USA, were black or dark blue and asking for help from 'Black Moriah' sounds very credible indeed.

*

Not long after leaving training school I passed my driving test and, after a police check test, I was eventually allowed to go out on patrol in my very own panda car. Properly, these were called unit beat patrol cars and I have been unable to find a really satisfactory origin of the 'panda' tag. Even Google (other internet search engines are available) doesn't help and lists references to being originally painted in pale blue and white. That could be why Chinese pandas don't do well outside of China; they're the wrong colour. It was a silly name, anyway. In theory, the driver would travel from the station to a remote beat, saving the time in transit, park up and walk around the area to be available to engage with the public on a face-to-face basis. It was a nice idea but it quickly fell flat because demand for response meant the driver just went from call to call during the day shift. At night, when there were fewer of us on duty, larger areas had to be covered. The need to double-up crews to deal with disorder further drew down on numbers and the panda became just another patrol vehicle.

Several makes of vehicle were used in the Met. Probably the most well remembered now will be the Morris 1000 but we also used Ford Escorts, Triumph Heralds, Austin Allegros and Hillman Imps. Personally, I only ever drove a Morris 1000 which I still believe is the most robust civilian vehicle ever produced in the world short of the Land Rover. (I once met a Morris 1000 in a high desert pass on the road between Tajikistan and Uzbekistan at over 2,000 metres where my Toyota Landcruiser was struggling for air.) From a police patrol point of view, they had the advantage of not being exceptionally quick. Fast cars encourage inadequately trained drivers, like me, to bump into things. They didn't corner terribly well at over about 15mph even on dry roads but could perform a most endearing trick which was very useful at night. Driving at 28mph in a brightly marked police car tended to cause a long line of frustrated drivers to queue up behind thinking they would be pulled over for exceeding 30mph if they passed. In fact, the patrolling driver just wanted traffic to flow normally while he or she checked for broken shop windows or things going on in doorways that were either illegal or too indecent for public display. The Morris 1000 could, when warmed up, be left to idle gently in first gear and would creep along at a dignified walking pace without stalling the engine. Slightly faster on a down-slope but needing just a little help on an up-gradient. I have no idea what this did to the life of the clutch but it seemed to work okay. Other drivers had the confidence to pass, it provided the visible presence that unit beat cars were always meant to supply and it was even possible to speak to pedestrians.

The only time I ever saw this technique create a problem was the night I was a passenger in a panda driven by Len in Camberwell New Road. Stopping to speak to two young men urinating against a lamp post, causing offence to others and danger of electrocution to themselves, they failed the Special Export Lager personality test and Len came round the car to join in the conversation. Unfortunately, he forgot to knock the lever out of gear and neither of us immediately noticed as it continued a solo patrol for about fifty yards before Len lost all dignity sprinting after it. My two interviewees had not quite finished what they had been doing and laughingly splashed their trousers. "Sorry, Officer. We won't do it again but you've got to admit, it was worth it to see that, eh?"

*

On a lonely patrol through the side streets off the Old Kent Road one dark night my Morris 1000 panda was having trouble if driven normally for more than about a mile but seemed to recover at very low speeds. After an hour or so of this, and concerned that I wouldn't be able to follow anything faster than a horse and cart, I parked up to investigate. I couldn't see anything alarming under the bonnet but could hear a wheezing sound coming from the rear. I even thought I had a puncture but the tyres seemed okay. Listening more closely I traced the sound to the petrol filler cap and when I took it off there came a grateful, sucking gasp from the tank where a vacuum had been developing. Problem solved. I carried on my patrol, stopping periodically to take the filler cap off and confident that no scrap metal dealer's horse and cart would get away from me that night.

Police vehicles were still a precious resource and reporting a defect which would take one off the road was not done lightly – guess who would have to walk until it had been repaired? The last job of any patrol was to top up the fuel ready for the next driver. The Morris 1000 had about a six-gallon tank but I could only squeeze about two gallons into it, so I left a note on it for the day-duty driver to get it checked in the workshop. It seems Morris had installed a petrol pump of prodigious power and when the petrol cap breather hole had become blocked the resulting vacuum had flattened the tank from a lozenge to something resembling a large, flat pie dish.

*

While the 'Moggie' was a very safe vehicle, no car is immune to bumps and scrapes especially when in the hands of a police driver. The 'POLACC' reporting procedure was tedious and involved the attendance of a traffic division supervisor – the much-feared garage sergeant. Hearing that an untraceable black cat had caused a police driver to clip a lamp post he insisted that he would mark the accident as 'to count', i.e. 'driver at fault', unless he saw the animal in question. While he was in the canteen the cat was found and left in the back of his pristine white Jaguar traffic patrol car. No one was able to explain how two pigeons also managed to fly in as well but they kept the cat energetically exercised until the garage sergeant had finished his break.

*

I enjoy off-road driving but don't get any particular thrill out of high-speed cars. After I bought a new car some years ago the dealer invited me to a demo day to try out some of their newer, faster models. It was great fun and even included some serious off-roading and a run around a motor racing circuit with a professional F1 driver at the wheel. But why would someone in marketing think I'd want to lay out £50,000 plus within a year of having bought one of their cars? All guests were given a Mountain Ash sapling to offset the carbon footprint of the day which I actually planted and now stands over ten feet high in my garden sheltering the greenhouse from natural sunlight. (Neither tree nor greenhouse can be moved.) I didn't buy another car and they've never invited me back.

In about 1970, I was the radio operator on Mike 3, a Jaguar saloon which, while not exactly designed for London's back streets, all our area car drivers seemed to love. At quite low speed we were passed by a Ford Escort, then among the most frequently stolen cars in the country, travelling in the opposite direction with four young men aboard. All four looked sideways at us then snapped 'eyes front' and accelerated hard. My driver, Eric, could drive his Jaguar backwards faster than most could drive forwards and had almost caught the Ford when its driver, foolishly, decided on a sharp right turn to get away from us.

In the back streets around the Elephant & Castle many of the roadside bollards were, in fact, old Crimean War cannon barrels, often eight feet long, sunk half their length into the ground and painted black and white. They tended to be unforgiving even to HGVs and a lightweight like a Ford Escort wouldn't even scratch the paint. The driver managed to hit one of these metal monuments to military might almost exactly in the centre of his front bumper leaving the headlights shining into each other and twisting the body so badly that the doors wouldn't open. This was unfortunate for the occupants because it was a two-door model and the driver had to endure a fifteen-minute road-safety lecture from Eric while we waited for the fire brigade to arrive – punishment enough in itself. On TV, no doubt the car would have been engulfed in a ball of fire. In real life, fortunately, that very rarely happens but the fire brigade still had the chance to try out some of their new toys to turn the car into an artistic arrangement of metal pieces and extricate the four completely uninjured young men who morphed from occupants to prisoners as they emerged. Their reason for trying to flee from us?

The driver had passed his test only the day before. The car belonged to his mother but had not yet been insured for his use and she didn't know he'd taken it. Outcome: a couple of minor traffic offences, huge bill from the fire brigade, one written-off Ford Escort. Total distance covered? Fifty yards.

Q-Cars

During the Great War the country found itself under threat of a maritime blockade but, being a seafaring nation, we had developed significant abilities in naval warfare which, combined with a natural British flair for sneakiness, resulted in the 'Q-ship'. These were harmless looking merchantmen which, when threatened by a hunting U-boat, turned into well-armed fighting gunboats. To use such a weapon in modern warfare might, arguably, constitute a war crime and be unthinkable. But that was back then…

Fortunately, such considerations did not apply when the Met decided to borrow the name, not to mention some of the glamour, to put 'Q-cars' on the street. The formula was simple; take an unmarked fast car, add a very highly-trained driver seconded from uniform duties for a couple of months, an experienced detective sergeant or detective constable and a third crew member who was invariably an aspiring CID officer. Freed from the day-to-day grind of investigating ordinary crime their only responsibility was to make arrests contributing to the honour of the division and the glory of the crew. A 'tour' would usually last eight weeks during which time their only competition would be the crew using the car for the other half of the day. They were even released from the tedious chore of claiming overtime and received 'Detective Duty Allowance' instead.

(DDA was a flat-rate payment calculated as an average of all overtime performed by CID officers and worked out to about five hours per month. It was paid to all CID officers regardless of whether they had actually performed extra duty themselves, including officers who never worked extra duty, such as some CO departments and those at training school. In practice it meant that divisional and operational CO department officers worked as required without other compensation. Usually everyone started at 9am or earlier and would not be expected to finish before about 10pm on several days per week. Court appearances, a frequent feature, were included even when assigned to night duty or special duty such as the Q-car.)

The division of labour between the crew was straightforward. The driver drove the car. He didn't get involved in dealing with prisoners or chasing felons on foot and rarely went to court. But the car had to be at peak performance when needed, clean and fuelled up. Periodically the driver would swap the vehicle for something equally nondescript but a stranger on the division. The DS or DC ran the team. As leader, his (never 'her') job was to make sure that intelligence sources were squeezed dry to produce the most arrests in the shortest time and he was reluctant to spend long periods on surveillance to produce a single prisoner – numbers mattered. The third team member (aid to CID, temporary detective constable, 'Scaly') was there to enhance his own reputation as a thief catcher, buy the teas and bacon rolls, make arrests, interview prisoners, take any necessary statements, apply for search warrants, do all the paperwork and present cases at court the next day – the Crown Prosecution Service was still in the distant future.

The team leader and the driver were experienced people of proven ability but a tour on the Q-car might only come around once or twice in a TDC's early career and could make or break a reputation. Taking leave was unthinkable. "If you don't want the tour, I'll find someone who does." It was not unknown for family holidays and weddings to be cancelled rather than miss a Q-car posting.

The call sign was always the divisional letter followed by 'One-One'. Mike One-One thus covered 'M' Division from downmarket Southwark, Carter Street, Tower Bridge, Rotherhithe, Camberwell and Peckham to upmarket Dulwich. Bravo One-One roamed around 'B'; Kensington, Chelsea and Notting Hill. This was a smaller area but was then, and probably is still now, one of the most socially, economically and ethnically diverse parts of the capital. Despite having such a large hunting ground and not just an assigned station area, the gov'nor wasn't usually too fussy about prisoners being arrested on another division, or even out of the Met area, provided there was a 'body' in the back of the log book at the end of the day.

As a young(ish) PC at Carter Street I'd been one of half a dozen officers called to a building site near Camberwell Green. Building sites have always provided rich pickings in terms of easily disposable scrap metal such as lead and copper or, in this case, phosphor-bronze fire-hydrant fittings. Having climbed the scaffolding and a couple of long, shaky ladders, I found Conrade and Borachio, eighteen years old – only a couple of years younger than I was but no longer 'juveniles' – trying to manhandle thirty-five kilograms of mains fire-hydrant down a ladder towards me. I let them sweat and strain for a while before uttering the mystical incantation "*Yer niqued*" which would keep them off the streets until Monday morning. (Similar spells to remove miscreants from circulation could be cast with, "*irishstoo*" and "*gottcha*" depending on the local dialect.)

On reaching the next down ladder I told Conrade and Borachio to go ahead because I could see a face I recognised below. This was Hugh Oatcake, a DS from my own station, who received them but as they reached the bottom of the ladder it somehow twisted and fell onto the scaffolding deck. It took me ten minutes to find another way down and then beg a lift back to the station where I arrived in time to see Hugh and the rest of the crew of Mike One-One booking in two young thieves to the credit of the Q-car. At least Hugh bought the teas and saved me the trouble of doing the paperwork. The Q-car crew had 'two for the back of the book' and Hugh owed me a favour.

*

No TV or film production about police can be complete without a car chase. American police cars are apparently manufactured without brakes at all so that they slam into each other at intersections and have suspension specially designed to send them barrelling in the air at the slightest bump. I've been a passenger in cars driven at eye-watering speed through London traffic and, yes, it is very exciting but the drivers need Zen-like concentration and find it exhausting. Advanced drivers have to know when to break off a pursuit in the interests of safety, or self-preservation, but an empty road is always inviting.

Just as Ginger Rogers did everything that Fred Astaire did but backwards in high heels, Q-car drivers did everything traffic patrol drivers had to do but without the help of sirens, blue lights or hi-vis livery on their vehicles. It takes another level of skill to scythe through heavy London traffic at 60mph in an unmarked car; that may not sound fast but try it sometime – on second thoughts, don't. My colleague Terry, a legend even among Q-car drivers, was driving Mike One-One in Tower Bridge Road one dark morning when he was passed by a Lamborrari Offashovel GTXE Super. Being a quiet sort of night, so far, he followed, getting up to 80+ when the DS team leader decided that the idiot behind the wheel of the car in front constituted an unacceptable danger to the public, despite all the fun he was giving them even at 3am on otherwise empty roads. They called for help from a marked car to help stop it when the driver realised that he was being followed not by three middle-aged men in a big car but by three middle-aged men in a police car. Speeds increased and more marked cars joined as the convoy wound its way from Peckham, through Sydenham and on towards Croydon. The nineteen-year-old driver eventually had enough and stopped in a lay-by to await what was coming and let his heart rate come back to somewhere near normal. A committee meeting around his vehicle concluded that further discussion should take place at the local station but the heated fast run had proved just too much for poor old Mike One-One, parked sad and neglected, on the other side of the dual carriageway. A wisp of smoke from under the bonnet turned to flames licking the tyres from under the wheel arches and soon the whole car was blazing merrily from end to end. Comment from the prisoner? "Don't blame that on me. At least I didn't set fire to my car."

*

Q-cars, although unmarked, were still pretty obviously police vehicles to the more astute and experienced felon. As a DC, and now the officer in charge of Bravo One-One, my crew and I were making our way very slowly in rush-hour traffic along Piccadilly – not strictly our area but not too far off. Our driver, Ron, had that morning swapped our superannuated brown Rover 3500 for a sleek new Vauxhall VX490 in dark green and he was ready for something he could legitimately use as an excuse to test his new car. About then a call advised all units in west London that three men had been seen in a green VX490 on the M4 heading westbound towards London, apparently aiming a pistol at other cars. The timing meant that they could easily be coming towards us from the Earls Court Road and we perked up a bit. By some miracle, traffic in both directions had ground to a halt as, on looking right, we saw a car almost identical to our own. The three occupants took an almost embarrassed interest in us then coyly looked away. Traffic was going nowhere so we got out of our car and made it clear that neither were they. Having caused a logjam in Piccadilly in both directions the whole of central London became gridlocked for hours (and we even had a mention on the news later that day). On TV, these young men would have been a team of professional hitmen on their way to carry out a contract. In fact, they were three juveniles from Cardiff who had taken a car from a station car park for a day out, fully intending to dump it in London and hitch-hike home. On the M4 one of them had looked in the glove box and found a very realistic looking replica Colt .45 which had frightened the hell out of them when they thought they had taken a car belonging to some major Cardiff mobster. (In fact, it belonged to a building society manager planning his Al Capone costume for the SW Regional Fancy Dress Dinner Dance.) No matter; three easy prisoners for the back of the book and hand it all over to south Wales. Ron was the only person upset as he never did get a chance to see what his new VX490 could do under pressure. It's sad to note that today even stopping the vehicle would involve deployment of armed teams and significant risk to the three kids themselves.

1966

In Memoriam

It would be wrong to talk about Q-cars without mention of the murders of the crew of Foxtrot One-One, namely Detective Sergeant Christopher Head, Temporary Detective Constable David Wombwell and Police Constable Geoffrey Fox in August 1966. In a street near Wormwood Scrubs Prison, they approached three men, two of whom were armed. The officers were not. One of the men shot dead DS Head and TDC Wombwell and the other killed PC Fox. All three were eventually arrested and convicted for the murder of the officers. One man died in prison in 1981; another was released in 1991. The third went on to become one the UK's longest-serving prisoners and was released, aged seventy-eight, in 2014. The murders have been the subject of numerous books and TV programmes including *No Answer from Foxtrot Eleven*[1] by author Tom Tullett who managed to get the call sign of the Q-car wrong. It was *Foxtrot One-One*, Tom, not *Foxtrot Eleven*. They deserve that much respect at the very least. I have used the correct names of the members of the crew who should be remembered. I prefer not to allow the murderers the dignity of mention by name; if you really want to know who they were you can look them up yourself.

---

1   *No Answer From Foxtrot Eleven*, Tom Tullett; published by Michael Joseph (1967).

IV

Detective Stories

1971

Please bear with me for a moment while I step back in time. By late in the eighteenth century Bow Street Magistrates had long been able to call upon their own force of Bow Street Runners to carry out duties on the authority of the chief magistrate. The area in which they operated was limited but, in practice, meant just about anywhere the chief magistrate said it did. Patrolling was undertaken only if businesses or residents in any given area were prepared to contribute to the cost. Quality varied.

The early formation of the Met was relatively simple. Home Secretary Robert Peel promoted the Metropolitan Police Act 1829 which brought the force into existence and empowered the first joint commissioners of police, Lieutenant Colonel Charles Rowan and barrister, Richard Mayne, who shared responsibility. Rowan was responsible for organisation and discipline and Mayne for legal matters. The area covered was broadly similar to today but specifically excluded the City of London which did not acquire its own police force until 1839 under a separate commissioner.

With the establishment of the new police came the appearance of 'Peelers' in their civilian-style uniform of tail coat, white trousers and tall top hat. (The hat had a copper lining on the top to prevent it rotting in the rain and hence 'Coppers'. Actually, that's one of several explanations but probably the most credible.) They were quite deliberately a highly visible presence to reassure the public and deter criminals; it still works today and is the reason why most police in the UK now patrol in bright yellow and not dark blue. However, uniforms hindered covert activity and in 1842 eight plain-clothes 'detectives' were appointed. The CoLP followed shortly after until, by the middle of the nineteenth century, most other major police forces had created some kind of detective or investigation unit or were in the process of doing so. In 1877 the detective branch was embroiled in a major scandal which almost led to it being disbanded but in 1878, soldier and barrister Howard Vincent was appointed by the Home Secretary to reform the branch into the Criminal Investigation Department. The new CID reported through Vincent directly to the Home Secretary until 1888 when the commissioner was again given responsibility.

Eighty years later, when PC Dogberry was on the street, it was usual for small teams of PCs in plain clothes to be put together whenever a 'crime' problem arose that the CID felt was beneath them – i.e. just about anything that involved going out in the rain – and the divisional superintendent could spare half a dozen PCs away from ordinary uniform patrol duties. Most frequently they were gleaned from the ranks of the night-duty relief and my name was always one of the first on the list of volunteers. Not that I disliked night duty, I just preferred to be out of uniform. Having established my reputation by making direct arrests for crime and serious violence, and showing commitment by not throwing my toys out of the pram when my Lightweight Motor Cycle Course had been given to someone else, I was approached by DS Oatcake, who I had met most recently on a building site when I was stuck on the scaffolding and he was in charge of Mike One-One. Hugh suggested that I consider putting in an application to become a temporary detective constable (TDC) and offered to endorse it himself. Contrary to popular myth, the selection process did not involve rolling up a trouser leg and swearing an oath at the point of a sword but was based on very transparent criteria and demonstrable role-related skills. I was interviewed at my divisional HQ by three senior CID officers I had seen but never spoken to, until I sat in front of them and came out fifteen minutes later thinking, 'Oh well, I can always try again next year'.

Earlier that week I had been seconded to another station on temporary assignment to the team handling what developed into a long, complex and sensitive murder investigation. It was my first proper 'murder squad' and very different from driving my panda on the 06.00 shift or walking the Old Kent Road in the rain. A couple of weeks later I was told my application had been successful and my career lurched sideways onto a new track.

*

The most important distinction was an invisible one that many uniform branch colleagues did not appreciate. The Met was organised under four principal departments at headquarters, Scotland Yard level, namely A – Uniform Operations; B – Traffic; C – Crime; D – Training. Over the years, other support branches and departments had been developed, such as Finance, Special Branch, Solicitors and the Laboratory, but those were the four primary Pillars of the Empire. By the time I left it had changed out of all recognition from that and is now an organisation which I do not understand at all.

However... police stations were then under the command of chief superintendents; they and all their uniformed personnel fell under A Department. What was not generally appreciated was that CID officers, even at divisional level were C Department personnel. Reporting and supervision went from the detective chief inspector to the detective chief superintendent at divisional HQ and from there direct to Scotland Yard. (Always referred to, by the way, as 'CO' for 'Commissioner's Office'.) Work was coordinated very closely between the two departments, of course, and proper respect was shown across the ranks, but CID officers were not under line command to the uniformed chief superintendent. This included TDCs, so my appointment constituted a significant change of role even though it did not mean a move away from the station. In future my boss would be my DS, through him the DI and DCI. I even had a new warrant card which had 'Detective' on it and handed back most of my uniform.

Strangely, because the job I was then doing on the murder squad was allocated for a uniform officer in plain clothes, and not a C Department officer, I was immediately returned to my station but not to my old relief. The glamour of the new status went off quicker than yesterday's milk as I joined the half dozen or so other TDCs working towards a permanent CID career. The day-to-day role was more like being an apprentice. We worked in pairs and were available to assist when extra people were needed for raids, executing search warrants or general office dogsbody. Paid overtime stopped and DDA became payable, effectively increasing the working week while reducing the pay.

The Detective Training School had moved relatively recently to Peel House where I had originally completed my basic training. I now went back there to go through a ten-week course in criminal law, procedure and forensic science training which was regarded as one of the best in the world. The standard was extremely high and law exams recognised as being at bar exam level. There were always several officers from other UK police forces on the courses as well as agencies such as the Royal Corps of Military Police and Royal Hong Kong Police. Later, on my 'advanced' course, there was a captain from the US Army Military Police who kept us all supplied with duty-free cigars; smoking in class was still compulsory.

For Met officers, failing the final exam was a career-ending disaster; it had been known but not recently. TDCs who had completed the course could now be allocated investigations and develop their experience. After the course it was also time to take the

Met promotion exam. Strictly speaking it was not absolutely necessary to be qualified to the next rank to become a detective constable but it was expected; certainly my DCI expected it. The Met then ran its own promotion examinations which were competitive. CID officers, however, waived their right to immediate promotion in uniform and had to apply later for selection for promotion to detective sergeant, a process which usually took another couple of years.

*

While I was still a TDC in darkest south-east London, I went with my colleague, George Seacole (I was now allowed to address detective sergeants by their first names) with a search warrant for a flat in an old local authority block, looking for new ready-made suits stolen during a factory burglary. It could hardly have been more simple and straightforward. The local resident burglar took a little while to open the front door but it was on the fourth floor and he'd had *Match of the Day* turned up very loud. We started to go through the flat while his mother made us all some coffee and insisted we have a piece of her delicious fruit cake. He was adamant that the twenty-five brand-new identical dark blue pinstriped suits in the spare room were all his and he hadn't noticed they were in a range of sizes none of which would fit him. A couple of hours later, with his solicitor enjoying his Saturday evening callout rate, he accepted that they came from the same factory where his father, now sadly deceased, had once worked. On Monday morning I went to court with him when he pleaded 'guilty' to burglary and the magistrate sent him for sentence to the Crown court. I sorted out the case file and forgot all about him, the suits, his mother and the address for the next seven or eight years until I was a DS in socially rocketing north London, where future socialist politicians would live in million-pound houses.

Going into what had once been a pub, but was now a tapas bar selling supermarket plonk at 750% markup, I met the manager lounging behind the polished black marble counter wearing a loose scarlet shirt, open to the waist to display a tea-saucer-sized gold medallion, spray-tanned chest and black leather trousers tight enough to need a health warning. He had a member of his staff beside him, similarly orange and almost wearing what I presumed was supposed to be a dress made of lengths of gold string of the kind used at Christmas to wrap presents. I didn't recognise him but his face lit up when he saw me. He told Jasmin, or it might have been Roxanne or Trixie, to pour a couple of glasses of wine and he even addressed me by name. It was necessary to prod my memory a bit but eventually it came back. He was, of course, the ready-made suit burglar from 'down south'.

In retrospect it had all been too easy at the time. Mum was uber-friendly and the fruit cake was really very good. He had even helped us to carry the suits to the car and admitted his guilt so quickly his solicitor had felt embarrassed to take a fee, but had forced himself to do so. At the Crown Court he had accepted a six-month prison spa holiday and was quite happy with the outcome. So why was he so pleased to see me? He relished telling the story which unfolded and enjoyed keeping me waiting as he let the suspense build. He reminded me that it had taken nearly five minutes to answer the door; I remembered that but still didn't think it too odd. What I should most certainly have thought odd, he said, was that his mother made sure we had coffee in the kitchen. Had we stayed in the flat's small parlour we might have noticed the fire burning vigorously despite it being a warm April day. We might even have been in time to see the remains of a stick of industrial explosive, which he had dropped in the grate a few seconds before letting us in the flat, fizzling to ash. I'm still not sure whether being told that made me feel better or worse; sometimes it's just better not to know.

*

After south-east London, elevation to the status of detective constable – and another new warrant card without 'Temporary' – had happened a couple of years later. My career had then turned towards the north and when the music stopped, in 1974, I was in Kensington, a station suffering from a kind of organisational schizophrenia. Apart from occasional forays over the river later on specific investigations, sometimes even armed and usually heavily escorted, I never worked on the south side again. (Among Londoners, sometimes even police officers but certainly between criminal gangs, there was then, and perhaps still now, a void between north and south London. These two tribal regions are not separated simply by a mere couple of hundred yards of dirty brown Thames river water but by a cultural gulf wider than that between the Klingons and the Vulcans.)

Police stations were then part of larger 'divisions', based more or less on local government borough boundaries. Southwark Borough was 'M' Division, with its HQ at Southwark Police Station, while the London Borough of Kensington & Chelsea was 'B' Division with an HQ at Chelsea Police Station. Unfortunately, Kensington had started to get a bit uppity and expansionist. Work levels were high and there were mutterings in the late 1960s of taking 'divisional' status away from Chelsea and passing it to Kensington which would have been rather like designating Romford as the capital of the UK. Please don't misunderstand me as I have worked in Romford and it is a very worthy place deserving of your high esteem but it just doesn't have the international gravitas of Westminster and I really can't see Her Majesty being too thrilled about moving to a council house on the Harold Hill Estate. Kensington went into therapy for a while and eventually emerged as two stations sharing the same building and designated BK 1 and BK 2.

I was assigned to BK 2 for two years during which time I met numerous people famous for being famous, television A-listers, lots of politicians and their various nieces (and nephews) and visited places where tourists just never get a chance to see past the front door. I was also one of the first to arrive at two bombings when completely innocent people were murdered in the cause of Irish Nationalism. Captain Roger Goad, GC, BEM, forty years old, Metropolitan Police

Explosives Officer, was killed by a bomb which he was attempting to make safe in Kensington Church Street on 29th August 1975. Professor Gordon Hamilton Fairley, DM, FRCP, forty-five years old, professor of medical oncology, was killed by a bomb in Camden Hill Square on 23rd October 1975. Both bombs had been planted by the same Provisional IRA active service unit; we were living in very interesting times.

*

But being a 'detective' had other consequences. Mrs Mabel Queen, an elderly relative of the future Mrs Dogberry, was not convinced that being a 'policeman' was entirely respectable. She knew the constable in her village was quite happy to turn-to immediately when her cat went missing – and was usually found behind the sofa nursing the latest brood of kittens – but otherwise there was no crime locally. It was some way from London, you will appreciate, but my visits to her classic rose-covered cottage still drew attention from her friends who could be relied upon to choose just that moment to urgently need to borrow a recipe book/icing bag/weeding trowel/copy of the *Radio Times*. One neighbour came in to ask whether Mabel could spare some coke to keep her going until her regular delivery came. (I didn't ask. She might just have wanted some fuel for the Aga but have you noticed how Miss Marple's eyes are always very red?) But to press on… The interrogation became quite probing during one visit until Mabel was asked a straight question, "And what does he do?" This came while I was out of the room but loud enough to be heard even without double hearing aids. Mabel had no real experience of uniformed services except for the Royal Navy but she knew I was not in 'The Service' and, even so, nothing less than a middle to senior commissioned rank would have been acceptable. She was, however, an avid who-dun-it reader, and knew that a murderer could only be brought to book by a suave, monocled sleuth from Scotland Yard who would clear it all up and be enjoying a dry sherry and the coy flattery of the widow of a recently deceased Spitfire pilot while the local copper was still licking his pencil. Problem solved then. To her friends, *sotto voce*, she confided, "He is a detective at Scotland Yard." Why was I in the village? Well, of course, she couldn't possibly say and enjoyed not possibly saying for months afterwards. At the time I think I'd been through the front door at Scotland Yard about five or six times and I'd even managed to address a civilian security officer as 'Sir'.

*

Television detectives are invariably accompanied by a 'sidekick' who is either barely literate or can lip-read fluently in Latin while simultaneously doing two crosswords in different languages. The exception seems to be DCI Barnaby in Midsomer, a rural area with a homicide rate high enough to depress house values and raise questions in the UN. Barnaby gets through DSs so fast I suspect Midsomershire Constabulary gets them from the local schools on work experience placements. However, he still manages to sort out whatever comes his way but is not averse to a little bit of illegal entry and search and miscellaneous other breaches of duty, law, discipline and conflict of interest which should have seen him fired, or worse, years ago. And am I the only person who's curious about how he manages to live in the style he clearly does on a detective chief inspector's salary?

If I disappoint you, I am truly sorry, but murder investigation is no different from any other scientific process of meticulous collection, collation and evaluation of evidence which is then presented to court. Pathologists do not lift fingerprints, take photographs, test firearms or interview witnesses and suspects. DNA does not solve every crime and it certainly can't be sampled, typed and matched within twenty-five minutes. The time of death is rarely more precise than some vague and unspecified time between when the victim was last seen alive and when the poor beggar was pronounced dead. Whodunit is often apparent from the outset; if it quacks like a duck and walks like a duck…

The only person who is *required* to accept the version given by the defendant, no matter how fanciful or obviously contrived, is the defendant's counsel. What makes murder investigation unique is that the victim, regardless of where in the social layer cake they came from, had friends, family and a future which has been taken away but that doesn't mean that some aren't a greater loss to society than others. Most crimes could be solved if the same level of resources could be poured into them and it would probably save more lives, and be more cost effective, to use the money simply to enforce speed limits but the public like to drive their cars fast and don't like the idea of murderers being left to roam. Former CID officers of my acquaintance will probably baulk at that idea – some of them having picked up the odd penalty point for having an overly heavy right foot.

V

More Detective Stories

1976

Fraud Squad

Kensington was followed by my first proper tour as a 'Scotland Yard' detective when I was posted to the Company Fraud Department – the Fraud Squad. Properly, we were the Metropolitan and City Police Company Fraud Department although we rarely saw our CoLP brothers because they didn't work in the same building. We weren't really even 'Scotland Yard' officers because we worked from a building at the back of Holborn Police Station which had previously been used by the police laboratory. I knew the department as 'C6', an abbreviation of 'CO.C6', later changed to SO6.

The same rules applied to our cases as any other investigation; gather the evidence by lawful means and let a court decide. It did not have the aura of dangerous mystery associated with such places as 'Special Branch' and the work was not nearly as cinematic. That said, I probably executed more search warrants and broke down at least as many doors while in C6 as I ever did later in the flying squad. But what we did do, and in spades much to the envy of just about every other department, was travel. There was rarely a week when I didn't get out of London to make a nuisance of myself in a company head office or town hall finance department. When inadequately trained and supervised people are given access to budgets that even today would look like a respectable lottery win, you must expect the mice to nibble at the crumbs.

Investigations in Wales were always a pleasure to take on not only because the scenery was a planet away from London but the people and police officers were invariably friendly and helpful and professional. But don't commute between London and south Wales in winter. The M4 is always wet and if you travel in the morning you will have the rising sun glaring in your mirror the whole way there and the setting sun all the way back. If you try to cheat and drive up the night before, you will be driving into the setting sun in the evening. I suppose you could always go by train if you have an extra day or two to spare and a really generous travel budget.

Over the next couple of years I visited every part of the UK, sometimes for more than a week at a time. The warmth of the reception varied markedly and not just whether I was offered a cup of instant coffee or not. Generally, I would make an appointment in advance to meet people high enough in the organisational food chain to give me access to what I needed and get things done. Sometimes there was a refusal to believe there even was a problem until I was able to show directors things like cleared cheques or purchase orders for goods they could not possibly need – such as a thousand years' supply of something with a three-month shelf life. On one occasion a town hall junior purchasing clerk was suddenly overcome with such a pressing need to check his car in the car park that he climbed out of the window but forgot his office was on the first floor. Sadly, suicide, attempted suicides and total loss of reputation, financial ruin, destroyed careers, marriage breakdowns and unemployment of whole workforces were not unknown. Fraud is not a victimless crime.

I managed only one trip outside the country during that first assignment but colleagues in other teams had office window ledges crammed with souvenirs from enquiries in the USA, Caribbean, Japan, Australia and South America. During an assignment to the fraud squad some years later the Russian Federation, which had recently become a full member of Interpol, sent over a small party of Moscow MVD investigators. These were the first law enforcement officers allowed out of the country to conduct an investigation since they had joined Interpol and it was important, for diplomatic reasons, that it should be a success. It was. We also looked after them socially very well and I still have the medal I was given when they left.

The term 'police' was not used by the authorities in Russia after the 1917 revolution because it was tainted by Tsarist era associations and loyalties and the Workers and Peasants '*Militsya*' was formed. In the USSR the Ministry of Internal Affairs or MVD (*Ministerstvo Vnutrennikh Del, Министерство внутренних дел*) was in overall control and the terms MVD and *Militsya* were, for all practical purposes, interchangeable references to what we would regard as civil police although the MVD, the ministry, also controlled fire-fighting and prisons. In 2011 the Russian Federation was leaning towards a more European image and there was yet another reorganisation in which the *Militsya* disappeared to be replaced by the *Politsya* (*Полиция*).

But things did not always go smoothly travelling abroad. A detective sergeant on another team found himself on a Caribbean island when a higher power tried to remove it from the planet and he ended up running the administration almost single-handedly until relief arrived several days later. On another occasion I sent a detective constable to the island where he had been born but the local chief of police saw an opportunity to recruit a highly trained and experienced detective and offered him a job. I can't blame him for wanting to stay; he sent me his warrant card and left me to explain to the commander how I had managed to reduce his already strained staff by one good officer.

1981

The 'Sweeney'

My two tours of duty on the fraud squad were separated by other CID postings, promotions and a couple of years back in uniform so I'm afraid you'll have to forgive me if this is jumping around geographically and in time but now would probably be as good a point as any to mention the flying squad. To insiders just 'the squad', it was formed in 1919 as a mobile unit of about a dozen detectives under a detective inspector tasked to deal with major crime across London without being confined by divisional boundaries. By the time I was assigned to it the correct title was the robbery squad but it's still known everywhere, including within the Met, as the flying squad with a remit to address organised armed robbery. (And we were very good at it too! I can really do no more than to refer you to some excellent books including *The Real Sweeney*[2] and *From the Flying Squad to Investigating War Crimes*[3] if you want to know more.)

Where did the name come from? Probably it was just a nod to the unit's quick response capability but it might also be a rather sneering jibe at their early motor vehicles which sometimes had to be push-started in Whitehall outside New Scotland Yard. The well-known nickname 'The Sweeney' derived from cockney rhyming slang for 'flying squad' (Flying Squad/Sweeney Todd). Since much of the early activity of the squad would have been against gangs from London's East End, and the teams of professional pickpockets which infested race meetings, some such criminal slang nickname would have been inevitable. 'The Sweeney' is probably one of the more polite terms that have been used from time to time.

When my daughter, Desdemona, was at university the old *Sweeney* TV series was going through a revival and had acquired a bit of a cult following among the student body. Desdemona had pinned

---

2   *The Real Sweeney*, Dick Kirby; published by Robinson (London, 2005) and other titles by the same author.

3   *From the Flying Squad to Investigating War Crimes*, Ron Turnbull; published by Pen and Sword (2019).

up a couple of extremely old photos over her desk, one of which was of me wearing a very wide tie, leather jacket and flares standing beside a mustard yellow Rover 3500 with a black vinyl roof, taken during a tour on the flying squad about twenty years before. It only needed DI Jack Reagan sitting in the car and the brassy *Sweeney* theme music blaring in the background. The other picture showed me in company with some very heavily armed jungle fighters in the Philippines. At a time when most of Desdemona's friends' parents drove blue Ford Mondeos or beige Vauxhall Cavaliers, I had a Land Rover 110. Dad had a bit of street cred but the kipper tie and flares were long gone.

I'm still not quite sure how I came to be transferred to the flying squad. I was a DS in north London and had expressed a wish to go back to the fraud squad (CO.C6) so a telephone call telling me to report to the commander of CO.C8 came as a surprise and I even checked to make sure someone hadn't misread the memo. The next two years can be best described as hectic while the team investigated all armed attacks on banks, building societies, cash-in-transit or other high-value targets. Suspects were identified as a result of good old-fashioned tedious police work, forensic science and closely controlled use of informants. Days and weeks might be spent watching a front door for a known 'face' to emerge or gangs of suspects to meet. No matter how TV has tried to present it, most of the time it was really very dull – until the end when a few moments of drama made it all worthwhile.

*

Usually one of the last things to do as any investigation neared conclusion was to obtain the search warrants we would need (DCI Barnaby, please take note, eh?). After six months of work the team collected one evening at a police station in east London. A decision had been made and we were briefed to arrest all our targets at 5am the following morning but we would need several search warrants. A search warrant can only be granted by a Justice of the Peace, a magistrate, on sworn 'information'. A couple of hours' two-fingered typing saw all the necessary forms completed and the 'on call' JP was contacted. It was very late but, "Yes, sir. It is very urgent and important." It was on my route home so while everyone else went off to get a few hours' sleep before the operation the next day, I drove to see the JP at home. He was expecting me and answered his door in an open-neck shirt, braces and carpet slippers but we were each a bit startled to recognise the other because this was my old headmaster from school, ribs long healed, now sixty and almost retired from teaching. What should have taken five minutes while I took the oath and presented the forms for his signature took much longer while he made bacon sandwiches and tea in the kitchen and we had a long chat covering everything that had happened to both of us since I'd broken his ribs.

My headmaster was Joseph Patrick Greene – JP Greene JP. Born in 1923 he had been just sixteen when the war started and through which he had come unscathed. An injury on an Italian beach a few years earlier would have earned him a medal but beach rugby didn't quite qualify although, I suppose, the Allied landings might have been a bit riskier. At the end of hostilities, he returned to life as a student to earn his BSc (Econ) as he began his teaching career, eventually becoming the first headmaster of the newly established school which I joined a year later in 1963. Looking back at my contemporaries from my school years I think JP should be given significant credit for producing people who were, generally, open-minded and ambitious. I telephoned him later in the day after our raids were completed to let him know that the searches had all been successful but, sadly, that was the last time we spoke. I don't know if there's a plaque to him at the school but there should be.

*

Being tasked to confront armed robbery meant that we took a lead role in just about every attack involving firearms. Not long after joining the team I was one of four officers sent to deal with three men arrested in north London. Two of them had entered a building society branch while the third waited outside. They had terrorised the staff and customers with a sawn-off shotgun before running out to their friend in the getaway car but had chosen a bad time as just at that moment a police car arrived and a chase worthy of any 'B' movie ran up through the division and into the park. There they left the road and drove through footpaths and flowerbeds past a very large ornamental pond where something was thrown out of the car window. Moments later they discovered what I could have told them about cast-iron Victorian lamp posts, namely that they were generally Ford Cortina resistant. All three were arrested. While my colleagues started to interview the three prisoners, I went to the park to see if I could find whatever it was they had thrown out. We had not found a shotgun in the car and the building society couldn't say if anything had been stolen until the security screens could be released.

The park keeper was very helpful. He had it on good authority from the head gardener whose son played for Everton (Boys) that something, maybe a large suitcase, maybe not, had been thrown from a motorbike, or it could have been a van, and had landed in the lake. How deep was the lake? Well, it had been dug to mark the Queen's Jubilee, Victoria that is, not the current 'er Majesty, and the councillors had spent a lot of money doing it. Nothing new there then. When it was drained to be cleaned out just before he had started to work for the council, after he'd had to stop working as a postman because he had a bad shoulder and couldn't carry the heavy sacks any more, he was told it was over twenty feet deep. A call to the Parks and Gardens Department suggested he might be a trifle generous with his estimate but it was certainly more than eight feet. I needed a diver.

The Met then ran the Underwater Search Unit which was part of Thames Division based at Wapping. They didn't usually turn out to emergencies unless there was a danger to life but, by chance, a search planned somewhere else had been cancelled at the last moment and I was able to get the services of a full diving unit. It impressed me and it impressed about a hundred of the local kids and even the TV news crew which had arrived just as the unit was setting up. The UWSU control vehicle, which I suspect was a converted horsebox that mounted branch didn't need, churned up the grass and would have been a huge problem had Everton (Boys) not been playing at home. A small dinghy was put in the water and tied off to a fence post. One diver was kitted out with a full dry-suit, breathing apparatus, safety lines, search tools and lights. His backup safety diver held the other end of the main line ready to go in at the first hint of trouble from his 'buddy'. I briefed them as well as I could on what they might be looking for and where it might have landed. A couple of test throws were even made by the sergeant in charge to see how far it was possible to toss a sawn-off shotgun-equivalent mass brick from a moving car ("Ford Cortina, did you say? Do you know what model?"). A last winning smile to the TV reporter ("Keep back, please. I do this for a living.") and he jumped into the murky brown water. I stepped back in anticipation of the splash but needn't have worried. The water, including the mud at the bottom, just about covered his ankles. A dry-suit isn't the easiest garment to walk in but less so through a muddy pond. By the time he had waded out to the island the water was around his knees and muttering could be heard about fatherless CID officers who should get a pair of wellies. The TV crew lost interest and even the park keeper decided he had duties elsewhere. After half an hour of rummaging around on hands and knees, up came a double-barrelled sawn-off shotgun. Or rather, the wooden stock of an old air rifle to which had been added two lengths of gas pipe attached with duct tape. Still, convincingly realistic and good enough, in due course, to add twelve months to the sentence.

VI

Bow Street Runner

1983

I left the squad after two years on transfer to Bow Street, probably the most famous police station in Great Britain. For me it meant a return to the basics of day-to-day crime investigation in central London – pickpockets, handbag thieves in the bars, sorting out the mess when Julian has smacked Gerald a bit too hard because he had smiled at Blair – probably accounted for ninety per cent of Bow Street's work. But there were also the usual assaults, murders and burglaries which mainly affected the relatively small number of people who were actually resident in the area all the time. Peter Stringfellow had the glitziest nightclub, in his opinion, a couple of hundred yards away but it wasn't a place I ever wanted to spend time in if I didn't have to. The Royal Opera House was directly opposite the police station front door but I got in there even less than to Mr Stringfellow's establishment. My time as a real Bow Street Runner didn't last long and I was transferred after about a year to the district crime squad at West End Central Police Station. The crime squad was an opportunity for uniform officers who wanted to come into the CID to show their worth as well as being a reserve supply of personnel for murder investigations, or anything else, when numbers were needed.

However, it was also time to get back to some serious studying and knock off the next promotion examination. After getting the pass I needed I was reassigned as DS overseeing pencil sharpening and coat-hook allocation until my promotion to inspector, back to uniform for the first time in many years and my first posting away from central London. I sometimes describe the next two years as being an assignment to the Far East which is not strictly untrue as Romford was as far as you could go in the Met before crossing into Essex.

After collecting my uniform, a great deal of that, I arrived to report to the district commander on my first day and received a briefing which lasted about three minutes before being passed on to Operations Chief Inspector Don John, who gave me a better idea of what was going on and where I fitted in. He clearly regarded me as a bit of a tourist, visiting the uniform branch for the minimum time before going back to the CID as a detective inspector. In truth, I really had no such intentions at the time and was looking forward to getting back to regular hours and out on the street again. After a couple of hours of wandering around the station introducing myself, and getting used to being called 'Sir' – we still saluted in those days – I found myself a desk in the inspectors' office and looked for a lift home. The control room kindly allocated a car to do this and my driver turned out to be Juliet Capulet, a PC who had only recently finished her probation. She chatted cheerfully and told me that I was to take over her relief, something the chief superintendent and chief inspector had either forgotten to mention or didn't know but she also managed to drop into the conversation that she'd been six years old when I joined the Met.

The relief had also been making some phone calls to find out about me which would only have been the sensible thing to do – I would have done the same and expected nothing less. If they assumed that having been in the CID for so many years I would be a bit green they were wrong but it was easy enough to let them know there was no trick they could pull that I hadn't done better a long time ago. We got on very well.

*

In the town centre was an abattoir serving the cattle farmers in the surrounding countryside. One bright, sunny day a young animal decided that being turned into burgers was not high on his agenda and jumped over a wall and into the car park (yes, cattle can actually jump quite well). He then trotted off through the town looking for a snack and causing traffic chaos. The call went to PC Capulet who followed the beast until it turned off the road into a football club training ground where it settled itself in the shade under a tree while Juliet wisely closed the gates and waited for help. I went along to make sure the abattoir staff sorted out their problem and found a couple of other police cars and a small crowd already gathering. The abattoir manager told me that the animal was a young bull and far too dangerous to approach so could I please get a police marksman to do the necessary job for them? Not as easy a thing to arrange as might be imagined but after permissions had been granted at all appropriate levels, we sat back to await the arrival of the nearest tactical firearms team.

Fortunately, the tactical team turned up quickly but seemed not to have been given a clear idea of why they were there as they all had full kit including body armour and helmets. I know bulls can be dangerous but I'm not sure they're actually likely to shoot back. Better briefed by me and the abattoir staff they looked at the problem again. There was no way anyone would get close enough to use a humane killer and a tranquilliser dart was not an option – the animal was just too big for anything that was readily available. They decided they did have something that would do the job but would need a close-quarters shot and two of them edged gingerly toward their target. The young animal had now wandered behind a screen of bushes and trees about 150 yards from the road and was happily out of sight of the swelling crowd and local press photographer. My cordon tape was still serving some use. After some minutes there came a loud bang, followed much to my surprise by a second. I was told later that the first had hit exactly the right place and knocked it off its feet. The only one more surprised than the bull was the officer who had just shot it when it got back up again, hence the second shot.

Show over and nothing to see, the crowd started to melt away. The local newspaper reporter took a couple of pictures of an empty field then saw Juliet standing by her car. Just what he needed, the young, blonde, photogenic lady officer at the centre of the *Mad Bull Shooting Drama*. As he went out, he asked one of her colleagues what her name was as he had forgotten to ask her. "Yes, of course, that's Emma, Emma Royds." She was not happy when she saw the local paper.

*

My station covered a mixed rural and urban area centred on an old market town, still cobbled and marked with post holes for the cattle pens. Time had changed local use, sadly, and a large night club with a totally inappropriate name, let's call it 'The Morons', had opened for business. After closing time one warm summer Friday night my van crew was called to a young man who had been found drunk, naked and handcuffed around a traffic light post, doused with about a pint of black gloss paint and white feathers. You've probably guessed; yes, he was getting married in fifteen hours and his 'friends' considered this was just the right way to end his stag night and abandon him in the street.

As his erstwhile friends had not taken the trouble to use standard police handcuffs, we had to get the fire brigade to come along with bolt cutters to free him. Much amusement all round there then but, fortunately for him, it was before the days of mobile telephones with cameras. The next morning's groom was now sobering up and becoming quite unjustifiably annoyed with us for his present predicament until it was pointed out to him that (a) it was his friends who had left him there and (b) that unless he modified his attitude he would not be getting to the church on time. Having unshackled our groom from the post, my van driver found an old sheet of plastic for him to sit on in the back of the van while they took him home. His timely thanks and an apology for his earlier lack of good manners had made the other possible destination unnecessary. I was told later that he might have found our charge room more welcoming than his mother's kitchen when she saw his condition and what she was now expected to clean up before the wedding. Someone managed to produce a gallon of white spirit and his mother and father set about getting their son ready for his nuptials. He probably also needed about a gallon of something to cover the pungent chemical aroma which I would think must have really made his eyes water and keeping lighted cigarettes away from him would, likewise, have been a good idea. I never knew what happened to his friends but we rather expected to be called to a disturbance at a wedding reception that night where the groom's mother had attacked six guests with paint and feathers.

Low-Speed Chase

During a night duty I was driving alone, thankfully not now in a panda, between two of the stations for which I was responsible, at about 3am when I found myself on a rural road behind a small hatchback crammed with what looked like half a dozen young bodies. The driver was not moving quickly. Indeed, it was his steady 15mph and six passengers that made up my mind to stop him and find out what was going on. Flashing the lights drew the attention of everyone in the car but the driver seemed unwilling to slow down, or indeed speed up. My commentary on what became a long low-speed chase was calm and leisurely and drew valuable suggestions from colleagues elsewhere such as commandeering an electric golf-cart or walking alongside and tapping on the driver's window. You can always rely on policemen for sound and helpful advice at times like this.

Even on cornering, the car's speed didn't vary much and the driver clearly didn't know the area as he was heading towards the town and one of my stations in the high street. Officers at the station had been alerted but had plenty of time to finish their snooker, tea and sandwiches and stretch a line of cones across the street which channelled the slowest fleeing vehicle in the Met safely into the car park of the leisure centre opposite. At 315am this was empty and the car just circled slowly with nowhere to go but with a growing audience of curious police officers lining the fence. The driver eventually found the brake but forgot about the clutch and kangaroo hopped to a stalled engine halt. The car was first approached by Liz, our dog handler, with Hero, a huge German Shepherd, which was giving every indication of having been fed on an exclusive diet of hatchback occupants. They refused to get out while Liz and Hero were there and I had to agree that I would have been just as reluctant myself. After putting Hero back into his van we managed to persuade six tearful children to get out. The driver, an elderly fourteen-year-old, had borrowed his neighbour's car because he knew where the keys were hidden. The youngest was just eight years old, and the only one to ask for a solicitor, but could look forward to a serious interview with Mum later. Outcome: no injuries, no damage, a couple of changes of underwear and, in due course, juvenile cautions all round.

1986

The Peasants are Revolting

Until the formation of organised police forces the duty of bringing individual miscreants to book fell to Justices of the Peace. This was still, often, a relatively simple matter as people tended not to travel far from home in the early nineteenth century and a JP was able to rely on a couple of constables, trusty stout locals with trusty stout cudgels, to make any necessary arrests. In any case of serious public disorder, a JP could call upon the assistance of whatever military unit happened to be garrisoned nearby to restore peace, uphold the law and arrest the ringleaders. Standards varied. In 1829 the Metropolitan Police Act had created a single police force for London under the control of the first joint commissioners of police who were themselves JPs. The Met area was a lot smaller then and was not extended until 1839. The City of London was excluded until the City of London Police Force came into existence in 1839. The Met and CoLP commissioners are still JPs today while the heads of all other police forces are chief constables.

In my experience, policing major public disorder involved getting wet, cold, and standing around for hours while otherwise reasonable people hurled abuse, among other things, at me in the belief that I was personally the cause of their pet peeve of the moment. I avoided it whenever I could. As a PC my training included tactics which would have been recognisable to Roman soldiers, linking arms in a wedge formation and pushing back against the crowd. You will have spotted the deliberate mistake, of course, which the Romans did not make. Lock arms with the two people on either side of you and you have nothing left to defend yourself and your helmet becomes available as a souvenir to whoever is immediately in front of you. The Romans would have laughed to see us doing this without shields, which were still a long way in the future, but perhaps it was a good thing that we didn't have short swords and spears. By the time police public order strategists had realised that ordinary uniform and a thin helmet made of cork were not fit for purpose I had hung mine up to become a CID officer and missed the delights of such later events as the miners' strikes.

Eventually, however, after finding myself back in uniform as an inspector, I couldn't dodge the public order column any longer. In west London the Met had built a training area with street fronts rather like a film set. Here we were trained in more modern strategy and tactics, use of shields, response to petrol bombs and entry and search of buildings. Some of these tricks I used later but most were just distractions. By now, the ladies had been fully integrated into all aspects of police work and trained along with us. The minimum height requirement had also been discontinued for both male and female officers but no one seemed to have told the company that made the long shields.

Years after leaving the Met I found myself working with a national police force a very long way from home. Discussing public order with them I was told by several senior officers, including a number of women, that whenever possible, they tried to ensure that the front row of their 'riot squad' teams included as many young, pretty female officers as possible, who would be told to make sure that their hair and make-up had been done. They would not wear helmets. This was apparently based on the theory that no man of their islands would ever be violent towards a woman. I was curious to know if the brick thrown from the back of the crowd was aware that it must not land on a recently coiffured female head and asked several junior female officers how they felt about it but they all thought it was quite reasonable. It's not a policy I would endorse.

*

One very long-running industrial dispute in London was the subject of almost nightly TV spectacles of riotous violent conflict between union pickets and their supporting crowds massed against ranks of police with plastic shields and rows of horses. In fact, except on a few regular nights of the week and even then, often, only in front of the TV cameras, things were relatively quiet. Sometimes five or six pickets would be outnumbered by police aggressively giving them cups of tea or snoozing threateningly in their buses in nearby side-streets.

On one such night I left my 'serial' (two sergeants and twenty constables) while I took a stroll to see what was going on elsewhere – nothing. Nearby I found five or six police horses with their dismounted riders by the catering van. (When this story is filmed they should be sitting relaxed around a campfire, drinking coffee and spitting wads of chewing tobacco – I want to make sure it sells outside the UK.) I chatted with the inspector in charge of them, not about the finer points of public order policing, we were both very bored with that, but about horses generally. I owned a horse at the time and very often rode in the rural countryside near to where the Romans had met Queen Boadicea, the original Essex girl but without the white stilettos. My colleague, let's call him Stan, offered to let me take his horse for a walk around the block and I mounted up happily. My uniform was broadly similar to his and I didn't look too much out of place; his horse was in fact a bit smaller than my own so I was quite comfortable. Off I trotted and had only turned two corners in this very dark area of industrial London when I met a deputy assistant commissioner, chief superintendent and chief inspector, all in full uniform, walking together towards the area where the police reserve coaches, including mine, were parked.

You should understand how unusual this was. Officers of this rank simply do not walk among mere mortals at night in full regalia and it would have been no more surprising to meet a bishop with an escort of priests, acolytes and supporting choir. I could hardly pretend not to be there so had no choice but to salute, offer a courteous acknowledgement and report that everything was "All correct, sir". I inadvertently pointed them the wrong way to the reserve coaches which gave me time to trot back to the mounted branch unit, give the horse back to his rider and warn him that the boss was on the way before getting back to my own bus. My serial hadn't even noticed I'd been away. Five minutes later three senior officers visited on their informal tour of inspection. The DAC looked a little confused but, I suppose, not having a horse made me look a lot shorter. The chief inspector smiled and told me that my team could 'stand down' soon. I got home about 10am and went out for a ride in the forest.

Over

When Career Development Branch eventually threw the Dogberry dart at the map of the Met after a couple of years, I again found myself in central London. The same round of issues arose but now from the elevated perspective of a detective inspector or acting DCI while my boss was away doing something else at the area HQ. Several murders, one major riot and a couple of world-class disasters later I returned to the fraud squad and, ultimately, my final assignment to the major investigation pool as a senior investigating officer based at Hendon, where it had all started over thirty-two years before. I know this goes in circles; it was making me dizzy too.

I've always enjoyed travelling and have been very lucky to have picked up cases in which travel to exotic places was necessary. A shooting, which became politically quite heated, took me to Ghana but that's a story in itself for later; for now, all credit to the DI on the team who had the whole thing wrapped up and charged by the time I came home.

When a complaint was made that a lady, buried in the Philippines, had been the victim of foul murder in the UK, Senior Investigator Dogberry, plus DS Benvolio, pathologist Count Paris, and forensics experts Friar Laurence and Friar Francis, travelled out to the Far East, i.e. well beyond Dagenham, to investigate. The details of the actual case are irrelevant but the trip was a very steep learning curve. For instance, I learned first that to exhume a body buried lawfully in the Philippines requires the authority not of a court but only the local office of the Department of Health. Even the local chief of police didn't know that. In the UK, exhumations are rare, and are probably becoming ever rarer as cremation becomes the method of choice for cadaver disposal. But if it has to be done, it's best, if possible, to do it in the early morning behind a discreet screen away from prying eyes. The local PNP chief was a rather flamboyant colonel who wore a nickel-plated, pearl-handled pistol at all times, on whom I tried my best to impress the need for sensitive handling of a delicate matter so I suppose I shouldn't have been surprised when I found a crowd of about a hundred people, reporters and a TV crew already at the cemetery when we arrived.

I came back to the island years later and met some of the people involved and the case was still remembered. The other significant thing to come out of that trip was the photograph which ended up on Desdemona's pin board at university.

And Out

I have never liked the idea that there is a separation between police and 'civilians'. In the UK, at least, police *are* civilians and policing, by definition, is a civil function so the word does not need to be qualified unless it is other than 'civil'. 'Military Police' is quite correct but 'Civilian Police' is not, as I've had to remind army officers, both at home and around the world many times. The term 'policing by consent' has real meaning but largely encouraged by TV drama and the news media, many people see police personnel as a species apart. I've often been asked about traffic enforcement policy or parking regulations, usually with a wink and a glance sideways as if expecting that 'something' can be done to sort out their latest speeding ticket. They then seemed amazed that I only knew what I saw in the papers. Would they think of asking a senior lecturer in dentistry about replacing worn bearings in their car's engine?

After more than thirty-two years of making a nuisance of myself in London I decided it was time to retire and start my world tour. And at least I wasn't asked about parking tickets quite as much.

VII

Off to War

1999

The Balkans – Kosovo

In 1998 the breakup of Yugoslavia was just about complete as the bloody civil war began to cool and new nation states, Slovenia, Croatia, Serbia, Bosnia & Herzegovina, and Macedonia emerged as the dust settled. In fact these were the old nation states from the early history of the region; some, such as Macedonia, were very ancient indeed. The dominant one, Serbia, was really all that was left over from the former Federal Republic of Yugoslavia, now simply known as Serbia, but included Montenegro and Kosovo. Probably because I'd had a holiday in Yugoslavia nearly thirty years before I'd followed what was happening in the region and at the end of 1998, I could do what most people in the UK couldn't; I could find Kosovo on a map and I knew the difference between Slovenia, Slavonia and Slovakia. Looking for something to keep me out of trouble after retiring from the Met I called a friend at the FCO and, after being passed through several other departments, I eventually found myself speaking in very positive terms about becoming a member of the Monitoring Mission then being put together to go to Kosovo. It was to be ten per cent funded, staffed and supported by the UK under the flag of the OSCE – Organisation for Security and Cooperation in Europe (sometimes, rather unkindly, also referred to as the Organisation for Spreading Confusion in Europe or Organisation for Starting Conflict in Europe) and would be called the Kosovo Verification Mission or KVM.

Since that first time I've done several assignments under a UK Foreign Office flag and their pre-deployment preparation is now very good indeed, including professional and practical first-aid training and off-road driving which is great fun but in 1998 the Kosovo mission was something new. A few days of battlefield awareness was hastily put together which included how not to get stuck in a minefield and how to get out if you hadn't been paying attention during the first lecture before coffee. Half an hour driving an army Land Rover, with Northern Ireland armour, and a 'Balkans Matrix' test gave me a MoD driving permit and there was just time to be issued with a pair of 1942 binoculars, map case, body armour and helmet plus some basic camping kit before being sent home. I sent my passport to Whitehall and sat back to await the call.

When the call came, just after Christmas, I felt that I had been cast in a cheap spy film. I was told to go to Heathrow and meet 'Rosaline' in the departure area who turned out to be very helpful and not at all 'Secret Service'. I still wasn't quite sure if I was in a TV stunt but anyone watching would have seen me being slipped a large brown envelope for which I had to sign. Rosaline vanished. Inside the package I found my passport, a copy of my contract, advice on packing – a bit late for that really – and a one-way ticket to Vienna leaving in an hour. The check-in desk was beside me and joining the queue I saw someone I'd met on the battlefield awareness course a few weeks before. At least now I had a destination and someone to talk to; so far so good. Neither my companion nor I had been to Vienna before and the instructions to that point only took us as far as flight arrivals but nobody was playing a zither or asked whether my grandmother drank only Turkish coffee on Wednesdays.

At an Austrian airport in winter it's not unusual to see travellers milling about wearing silly hats and carrying long bags of skis. Not being a great fan of broken bones, I've always avoided skiing but on this day I felt quite properly dressed as most people around me in the arrival hall were carrying, one even wearing, body armour, helmets, rucksacks and lost and lonely expressions. In the detecting trade we called these things 'clues' and I noticed them instantly. Well, I noticed them after about fifteen minutes when a taxi company rep asked if I was with the OSCE party. Two minibuses took us to a hotel in the city centre where slick Austrian administration had us all checked in and rooms allocated in about five minutes. I can't remember whether anyone wanted to find a restaurant but the hotel bar did very good business that night.

*

The headquarters of the OSCE was in the very grand Hofburg Palace in the centre of Vienna. Well, not the whole palace and the actual entrance was a little side door but the address impresses tourists. It's somehow always a pleasure to walk through a door marked '*Einreise absolut verboten*'. The next three days were described as 'training' but were really administrative checking to make sure everyone had the correct papers, stamps on documents, medical clearances, personal kit and some idea of why they were there. Standards of preparation between countries varied enormously – the UK was certainly the best. A dozen of us had arrived more or less together, knowing what we were going into and properly equipped and, as far as could have been done in the time, adequately trained. But if we set the standard, very few others reached it. Mission members from the USA and most European countries tended to be military or police personnel on secondment who came generally quite well prepared but there were exceptions. Ursula, a lady from Europe – I won't embarrass her or her country of origin – had to go shopping as she had come for deployment to a war-zone with no footwear other than four-inch heels. Vienna is a lovely city and the schedule included lots of time to sit in open-air cafés in the freezing January sunshine enjoying *Sachertorte* and hot chocolate with rum. Oh, there were some lectures about Kosovo as well but nothing too taxing. After we had been assembled, papers checked, rechecked, photographed, issued with OSCE identity cards and papers checked again, we were allocated to flights from Vienna to Skopje in Fyrom.

*

I think a word of explanation about Fyrom might help here just to confirm I was actually in Europe and not with Dorothy en route to Oz. In 1991, with the beginning of the disintegration of the Federal Republic of Yugoslavia, Macedonia had declared its independence and that it would be known henceforth as 'The Republic of Macedonia'. Greece objected on the not unreasonable grounds that Macedonia was the name of a region within their sovereign territory. I can imagine a similar reaction if Brittany declared independence from France and decided that in future it wished to call itself 'The Republic of Devon'. But more than just national pride was hurt and there were fears of revolution spreading south and the stench of burning tyres on barricades was already in the air. Like a pop star, the newly minted, independent nation might have opted to use an unpronounceable symbol as a name, but instead just went along with 'The Former Yugoslav Republic of Macedonia' temporarily. Always reduced in print to the acronym 'FYROM' it was not long before it was used as a spoken word, i.e. Fyrom, pronounced 'fierum'. To this recipe for total confusion was added a little spice of local accents and the fact that it was not shown in the index of any atlas. Fyrom and Greece each accused the other of being terribly rude and nasty at the International Court of Justice but an interim solution seemed to be that Fyrom might be known as North Macedonia. Until this was resolved the Hellenic Republic showed itself willing to sit in the corner and hold its breath until it turned blue while

Fyrom declared a readiness to suck its thumb until such time as an acceptable compromise had been reached, i.e. it had got its own way. Membership of NATO, admission to the EU and participation in the Eurovision Song Contest turned on these things. The last time I checked, 2019, after deliberations at the ICJ, EU Parliament, UN (and possibly the admissions committee of the Eurovision Song Contest), innumerable meetings, conferences, high level and informal talks, it had been proposed that Fyrom would become the Republic of North Macedonia. There is probably more mileage yet in this saga but, as we are still talking about things as they were in 1999, I shall just refer to it as 'Fyrom'.

*

This was a period when hardly anyone went to Fyrom except to go on to Kosovo. Our flight arrived late in Skopje on a dark evening during a lightning storm of biblical extravagance. The runway aims directly towards a very solid looking mountain which I presume regular pilots have been advised to avoid. Our pilot seemed to enjoy the approach so much he did it twice, even getting his wheels briefly on the ground at one point. I always find information from the flight deck very helpful but there's something a trifle disconcerting when there is just a bump and the captain says, "Oops". He was just coming round again when all the city lights went out, including the runway lights, and we were told there had been a power cut. Having made a couple of abortive attempts to land, and seeing no chance of either power on the ground being restored or a let up in the weather, we headed back to Vienna. Safely on the ground at the terminal we collected our bags but since we were now the airline's problem we were taken to a much nicer hotel close to the airport and told to be ready for a flight next day at 07.00.

We must have looked a bit odd. Everyone was dressed in various styles of camouflage ranging from the very latest US 'chocolate chip' desert kit (as worn by discerning special-forces personnel everywhere) to French 1914 vintage, including knee-high puttees. Even Ursula, our lady with the stilettos, had managed to find someone in Vienna who had not only sold her some more suitable, but no less chic, footwear and clothing but had even had it tailored and fitted – the sort of service usually only available in Bangkok. All badges, decals and rank insignia had been removed and we were probably liable to be arrested as insurgents or spies. In the hotel lobby we mixed with ladies wearing gowns which probably cost more than all of our kit combined and their elegantly black bow-tied partners who looked at us as if Austria had gone to war and they hadn't been invited. The hotel bar did another good night's business and we reassembled at seven o'clock in the morning. This time it was a direct flight in brilliant sunshine to a smooth landing in Skopje. We were almost there.

*

By now the new monitors group was getting larger and more international. OSCE member countries include the USA and Canada, Mongolia and The Holy See pushing the limits of Europe even further than the Eurovision Song Contest. After sunset, forty of us got on a bus in Skopje to be driven over the border into Kosovo, a ride that took about forty-five minutes. At the border we were checked out by the Fyrom border police and crossed a no-man's-land gap to be looked over by the Serbian border police who went through our papers, checking every page of every document with meticulous care taking something over an hour altogether. The storm had returned and the mountains added snow making the remainder of the trip great fun; fun in this case is defined as meaning a bus ride at night on unlit, untreated roads through the mountains in a blizzard.

The next stop was a hotel where the KVM/OSCE had established a forward training base and where we would spend the next few days. Probably the most important thing to do was to take and pass the

OSCE driving test to show we could drive a 4x4 in a straight line for about half a kilometre. Even so, these were manual transmission vehicles and there were one or two people who had only ever driven automatics. ("Say! What's that other pedal for down there?")

Our transport mainly consisted of Jeep Cherokee 4x4s with retrofitted ballistic panels in the doors and bulletproof glass. (Don't believe it – nothing is really bulletproof.) This generously proportioned car had to carry four people wearing rucksacks and body armour, including a helmet, with inside dimensions reduced to something like a Ford Anglia. Part of the US contribution was to supply the mission with several military 'Humvees'. The High Mobility Multipurpose Wheeled Vehicle or HMMWV, always known colloquially as a Humvee, is manufactured by AM General for US military forces. The civilian version with high-gloss paintwork and chrome-plated trim is a 'Hummer' driven by drug dealers, film stars or people pretending to be either. We had the military light-armoured variant which meant that the passenger cabin was made of solid steel plate with a Kevlar rear section about an inch thick and a laminated glass windscreen two inches thick. Wearing a helmet inside was vital as there were lots of hooks, latches and other odd projections on which to leave a blood sample. These were enormously enjoyable to drive until an instruction came to us that only US personnel were to drive them. At my location we had been assigned two Humvees but only one US mission member – and until another was assigned we got by on the principle that it's easier to ask for forgiveness than permission. The British, not to be outshone by the USA, had supplied several army Land Rovers which had been reassigned from duties in Northern Ireland. These had the same level of ballistic protection as the Humvees, and were a lot more comfortable to ride in, but were, basically, standard Land Rovers with bigger engines, uprated brakes and suspension and a couple of tons of armour. The result was a vehicle with the acceleration of a milk-float and stopping distance of the Ark Royal which would sink when driven off road onto mud, unlike the Humvee which was wide and low and even the tyre pressures could be readjusted from inside. The Land Rovers were all allocated to other areas, however, so I only ever had to use the Humvees and Jeeps.

*

The hotel which the KVM had taken over had formerly been a state-run tourist hunting and skiing resort. Decor was in 1975 primary colours, lots of orange, yellow and blue, which had clearly never been renewed, or in places even wiped over with a damp cloth. Lots more forms had to be filled out and I later found out that a lot of what had been provided in Vienna hadn't been passed on apart from a list of names of new arrivals. After the OSCE driving 'test' there was instruction in various new hi-tech toys that some of us had never even heard of, such as personal GPS and satellite telephones.

There were two versions of the sat-phones. The vehicle version – meaning only available in Humvees – was a large piece of equipment built into the overhead panel in the centre with an antenna wired through on the roof. They always worked but needed a few moments to find a satellite. The portable version was built into an attaché case and looked rather like the sort of kit spies would have used at the time but we laugh at now.

- Open the case on a firm, level service and switch on to check battery state and signal strength.
- Find somewhere to recharge the battery.
- Deploy the antenna, which looked like a miniature folding radar dish about twelve inches across made of kitchen foil, then use the handy pocket guide to find the approximate position and angle of the nearest satellite.
- Fine tune the antenna alignment and log on to the system.
- Make a call hoping that a dark cloud doesn't cover the sky or the battery go flat before you're finished.
- Give up and find a hotel or bar with a working telephone.

- Just give up and be content that you've found a hotel with a bar.

Today, a mobile telephone, smaller than a bar of chocolate, with built-in sat-phone access makes seamless calls using whatever system is available.

*

Accommodation was cramped and I shared a room with an Italian Marines reserve captain and a British Royal Air Force regiment lieutenant. The room had been a children's bedroom in a family suite and was hardly adequate for three men with a lot of personal kit. All the staff were ethnic Albanian and regarded us with extreme caution which I thought was a bit unfair given that it had been the political representatives of the Kosovars who had pressed so hard to have us deployed in the first place. The hotel had been designed with cost in mind. There was a lift but it only held two people, or one person and luggage and had no inner door so best not to lean back. The central staircase wound around the lift shaft but had steps only as far as the first floor, after which it was a steeply rising smooth helix. It was probably great for a bit of ski practice coming down but a climbing rope would have helped a lot going up. After about a week we were sent to Pristina to await deployment and transport.

I was assigned as deputy director at a 'reporting centre' in the south of the country. Even now, I really don't feel this is the place to go into a lot of details of what was happening. Civil war is the most brutal kind of conflict and the whole period of the disintegration of Yugoslavia was marked with atrocities perpetrated by one part of the population on the other. Each side justified what they did with, 'They do this to us, so we will do it to them', citing battles and events hundreds of years ago. At the Battle of *Kosovo Polje*, meaning 'Field of Blackbirds', in 1389, Serbian Prince Lazar fought the Turkish forces of Ottoman Sultan Murad I. Both leaders were killed but the referees awarded the contest on points to the Turks resulting in the collapse of Serbia and 600 years of mutual bitter animosity.

*

Having been assigned to a base location we were mainly engaged in setting up the administrative structure of what was thought likely, at the time, to be a very long-running mission. We had to establish a confidence building presence on the ground from the main office and at the same time had to find, rent and furnish two more field offices in remote locations. As soon as we could we started to run highly visible 'patrols' around a very poor, war-damaged country while diplomatic talks were taking place just outside Paris at Rambouillet.

A 'patrol' usually consisted of two 4x4 vehicles with crews of either two or three in each. The theory was that there would always be one vehicle to rescue the other if need arose but really it was so that there were plenty of people to push when one vehicle bogged down, although there were a few team members who were reluctant to get mud on their gleaming boots or immaculately tailored camouflage kit. Poor Ursula sometimes still believed that she should be able to go out with a team wearing four-inch heels and a skirt so tight she had to take care to preserve her modesty. Another newly arrived member was so huge that he couldn't get in any of our vehicles while wearing body armour, a non-negotiable requirement, and complained to his ambassador when he was not allowed to join a patrol. New personnel arrived from KVM HQ in Pristina almost every day and it was difficult to keep ahead and simply find temporary accommodation. "Sorry, your problem. Send transport for another four tomorrow." I would usually send one vehicle to Pristina just for four new people plus a back-up to carry kit and for any extra passengers who needed to visit the headquarters for meetings – or have a pizza. If the new arrivals were German soldiers it meant sending two extra vehicles because they would always turn up dragging huge metal boxes with their kit. I then had to explain to HQ operations that I hadn't sent out any patrols that day because all my spare vehicles were tied up running a taxi service.

My area included some of the most interesting terrain in the country where the rebel opposition was the Kosovo Liberation Army (always referred to as the KLA or by its Albanian acronym UÇK for *Ushtria Çlirimtare e Kosovës*) which was a separatist militia that sought separation of Kosovo from the Federal Republic of Yugoslavia and Serbia and the eventual creation of Greater Albania due to the presence of a majority ethnic Albanian population in the region. The KLA was engaged in waging a skirmishing war with the official Serbian 'Special Police'. Such 'police' forces were a feature of most former Soviet-type administrations and were usually distinguished by heavily armed mobile units in which line command was through the Ministry of Interior, or even directly to the president, rather than to the minister responsible for the army. In Russia they were then called 'Interior Troops'. 'Specials' in the UK don't get assault rifles and mortars – well, maybe in Stevenage but not anywhere else.

*

One day, working our way along a mountain track we could hear automatic rifle fire ahead being answered by machine guns. There is a significant difference between the two which it's a good idea to learn if you wish to stay around long enough to learn anything else. We were not equipped to go into this kind of situation – getting shot can ruin your whole day – so we just recorded the location and turned round to report back. Coming down from the hills we met a group of villagers walking along the treeline obviously also trying to stay away from the fighting. The group was comprised mainly of women, old men and young children. The Serb Special Police were always on the lookout for 'terrorists' and any man, or boy over about fourteen, was regarded as suspect. On seeing us, the villagers started to scatter despite us calling to them in English to let them know who we were even if they didn't understand what we'd said. They were frightened because they had a twelve-year-old boy with them and if we'd been the Special Police he would certainly have been arrested. Their problem now was to get to the next village but they knew there was a checkpoint on the road.

My colleague, Frank Seacole, a former US soldier from Kentucky who could spit wads of chewing tobacco five yards with deadly accuracy, agreed that letting the boy stay on the road would invite trouble so we buried him between the front and rear seats of our 4x4 under a pile of coats, rucksacks and food rations. Half an hour later at the checkpoint the sergeant in charge was confronted by two bright orange 4x4s carrying a very uncooperative bunch of foreigners. No, we would not allow him search our vehicles, they had diplomatic status, and no, we did not wish to speak to his captain. If anyone at all was to be called, it should be no one less than his colonel. We were unarmed but a demonstration of ballistic expectoration can be very intimidating and a Brit being as arrogant as only a Brit abroad can was too much. I have no idea what his parting comment was precisely but I don't think it was an invitation to visit again soon. We dropped off our hitch-hiker an hour later in the village. I have no way of knowing if that child made it through the conflict but at least he made it off the hillside that day, which was a start.

*

I became used to the kind of village from which these people had come. Generally, Serbs in Kosovo lived in the larger towns while people in the villages, usually ethnic Albanians and mostly Moslem, lived a much simpler rural life. The Serbian Special Police were probably correct in their assumption that most Kosovan men were KLA members or supporters. In some cases, villages were entirely empty of men except for children and the very old. The winter was harsh in the mountains in 1998/99 and movement, suppressed by the conflict, poor roads and the absence of the menfolk, caused hardship which people who have not been in such conditions cannot really comprehend.

Our patrols were planned for daylight hours, roughly 08.00 to 18.00 but we always carried at least three days' supply of emergency rations, water and first-aid supplies. We had US Army and British Army field ration packs which were varied and very good. We also had Norwegian emergency rations which consisted of a type of large high protein, high fibre, high calorie biscuit and, of course, we always had chocolate. This would keep you alive – you might even pile on weight over time – but you would be very happy to get back on real food. If we got ourselves into trouble we had to get ourselves out. It's a standard rule of working in these kinds of environments that you do whatever is possible to help but you don't give away your own emergency rations or your personal first-aid kit especially the tourniquets and morphine. There's no point in simply becoming one more problem for someone else to solve.

Arriving in one village in the hills one morning we felt helpless when we found people who had not eaten for several days. The Special Police had left them alone for weeks but the villagers were down to burning furniture to keep warm. Our ration packs represented more food than this village had seen in a long time and there was a mutual acceptance between the patrol team members that there was only one thing we could do. There were six of us and therefore eighteen days' worth of food at 'field' rate of use so everything was opened up and shared out. Probably enough to keep them going for nearly a week. While this was happening, one of the team noticed that we had given away a couple of packs of pork stew (with red pepper sauce and vegetables) which was going down very well too. When the village Imam noticed that we were looking worried it was explained that we had made a mistake. He spoke a little English and understood our dilemma but didn't spend long thinking about it. "In time of need, Allah will understand." Probably one of the most sensible and pragmatic things I've ever heard from a cleric of any religion.

*

I worked with Frank quite a lot. He turned up unexpectedly, but most welcome, about three years later in Sudan but that's another story for later. He was also with me one night when we were out 'monitoring' an army base in the area. Sometimes the army would decide to have a bit of fun and take three or four tanks out for a romantic moonlight ride. This not only made sure all the villagers were kept awake but it churned up the roads making them almost useless to civilian traffic and even our 4x4s could only get round with difficulty. Frank and I were in a Humvee which we parked on a rising piece of ground opposite the main gate of the base. We were not exactly low profile. The silhouette of a Humvee is unique and we had the moonlit sky behind us. The vehicle was painted bright orange, with a huge flag and a light on the roof. This was going to be a long night if the tanks stayed in the base. After an hour Frank pulled down the sat-phone handset to make a call. Satellite telephones look just like ordinary mobiles today but were then very new technology and I had never seen one used before. I knew they were hugely expensive and charges of about $30 per minute were talked of. Frank's call lasted about an hour after which he passed on regards from his wife in Kentucky who had been on the other end of the line. He told me that all US military vehicles, ships and aircraft had a sat-phone but there was only a single combined bill which, apparently, could not be broken down to specific units. "Would I like to call home?" Of course, I would. I remember the date exactly because it was my birthday and when I got through to a very surprised Mrs Dogberry my birthday party was in full swing. I talked to some of my neighbours and other guests some of whom, even today, insist that they saw me at the party – but I know I was on a hilltop in the snow in Kosovo. I would just like to say thank you to the US Defense Department for letting me make the call but don't even think about sending a bill.

*

Unfortunately, shortly after the talks had been arranged it very quickly became apparent that it was not quite going to plan. After a massacre at a village in our area in the south of Kosovo the talks in Rambouillet collapsed and the whole mission withdrew not long after in a single column back to Skopje in the snow in a single day. It was my first experience of an exercise in military-style organisation and I was very impressed. The entire mission, around a thousand people and vehicles, came across the border in a single convoy in just a couple of hours and took over two hotels which were delighted with the sudden rush of trade. My group was eventually moved down to another hotel at Ohrid where the border between Fyrom and Albania runs through Lake Ohrid. Now and again there was a need to drive to Thessaloniki to drop someone at the airport but otherwise it was a very tedious time while we waited to see whether an agreement might yet be salvaged and we could go back.

Behind the hotel was the sort of mountain that children draw – just a straight-sided cone with snow on the top. Really it was just a very steep hill but it was a mountain to the local people so they should know. One bright morning four of us decided to climb it. It was a well-planned expedition taking food and water, first-aid kit, map and compass. The path led more or less straight up and we felt pretty pleased with ourselves getting to the top in one go and deserved a good lunch. Our party of explorers consisted of me, over fifty, overweight but reasonably fit, a thirty-five-year-old ex-Royal Marine, an army reserve officer and a sergeant from the RAF regiment on secondment. No problem but I have to say even my younger, fitter, colleagues found it challenging. Although still only early spring it was warm and we were all ready for a rest at the top. What we weren't ready for was meeting a very elderly lady walking up the mountain from the other side where she had obviously been at the village market and was now heading home. This frail-looking lady, dressed head to foot in black, was carrying a large and obviously very solid kitchen table and two baskets while I had a packet of sandwiches and a bottle of water. Don't mess with Albanian ladies; they're tough.

We mounted our own night security patrols at the hotel and it was while walking around in the dark with a former US police officer that he pointed to the 'aircraft' crossing the sky without navigation lights. They didn't need them – they were cruise missiles on their way to Kosovo at the start of the invasion. We would not return and were all flown home a couple of weeks later. I haven't been back to Kosovo since.

VIII

"Closed. Come tomorrow"

1999

Croatia

The contract I'd signed for Rosaline at Heathrow had included a clause about remaining on standby and I was quite happy to withdraw to Devon and await the call. I watched what was happening in the Balkans with some interest but didn't really expect to go there again. I was very pleased, therefore, when the Foreign Office called me and asked whether I would like to go to the OSCE mission in Croatia. This had been running a lot longer and was the model for what the Kosovo mission might have been like if things had held together politically. There was the same pre-deployment paperwork to do but at least this time I had already done the driving, first aid and minefield training and had all my kit ready packed.

I flew to Vienna again for induction lectures and endless form-filling but this time three of us were driven overland from Austria to Zagreb by taxi. A quick visit to the OSCE mission HQ, where yet more forms had to be filled in, was followed by a meeting with the deputy head of mission. I then continued my journey by car to Vukovar but this time with just a driver for company as my two newly-arrived travelling companions had been assigned to other places. It turned out to be a very long day on the road but it was a good way to travel and see the country. Vukovar was one of the regional HQs and is in the east where Croatia is surrounded on three sides by Hungary to the north, Serbia to the east and Bosnia & Herzegovina (BiH) to the south. The war had been over for several years and Croatia was recovering and working toward EU membership (and Eurovision Song Contest participation). In the east there were still obvious signs of the fighting which must have been intense. Some buildings had been so blasted by small-arms fire that they seemed whittled away to almost nothing. Electricity pylons just lay in the fields and a motorway flyover had simply been severed with explosives at each end and left lying by the road.

Much of the open land was contaminated with landmines for which there were no proper plans. Landmines fall into two broad groups. 'Anti-tank' mines are designed to take a main battle tank out of the fight and usually consist of a buried box containing about 15kg or more of high explosive which can lift a fifty-ton vehicle ten feet in the air. Usually pressure activated, they are designed to destroy vehicles, not just one soldier, and therefore require a lot of pressure to set them off. 'Anti-personnel' mines are much smaller and concealed in devious ways to be set off by pressure, trip wires or even the vibration of someone passing nearby. They are designed to cause serious injuries, not necessarily kill, as the enemy must then deploy resources to bring an injured soldier out of the battle. They also damage morale and deny territory to the enemy. Unfortunately, they usually can't tell the difference between a soldier, a passing goat or a child. Some are even improvised but just as deadly and contaminate the battlefield for years.

*

After being greeted in Vukovar I was sent on to Osijek, about twenty-five miles north of Vukovar, which was to be my base for almost the next couple of years. Apart from a few 'splash' marks where rocket-propelled grenades had hit buildings, most of the damage from the conflict had been tidied up and swept under the corner of the carpet. The Osijek Hotel boasted a lift which actually worked and could carry six people. Balkan men and women tend to be quite tall, something I have never been accused of, however, coming down for breakfast next morning I found myself riding in the lift with two men and two ladies, not two couples, just guests but who appeared to know each other. The shortest of the women was about 6'1' and the tallest man about 6'8' making me feel like a garden gnome. More towering guests were having breakfast so I just had some rolls (fresh and extremely good) and coffee (stale and so weak you could see the bottom of the cup) and resigned myself to a couple of years of diminutive toil. I had a good street map and my office was only a five-minute walk away and it was a sunny autumn morning so I enjoyed a walk to work in the Land of the Giants.

The HFO (Head of Field Office – the OSCE, like all international organisations, loves to use acronyms whenever possible to confuse outsiders) was a Bulgarian diplomat named Zoltan and was one of the most professional, experienced, helpful and pleasant people I've ever worked with. He had been educated and trained as a diplomat in Moscow in the days when Bulgaria was under very heavy control from the USSR. Apart from his native Bulgarian he spoke fluent Russian, Serbo-Croatian, English and French. Unless it was extremely hot, which it can be in Eastern Croatia, he usually wore a black cloak fastened with a heavy brass chain, a wide-brimmed black hat and carried a black silver-topped cane in flamboyant style with confident panache. In his office was a large dome-topped bird cage wherein lived an ancient red, green and black parrot with an unpronounceable Bulgarian name so let's call her Polly. The cage door was always left open and Polly would wander in and out at will, even sometimes taking a quick, noisy flutter to perch sideways on the chains from which the lights were suspended. It was an old building with high ceilings and if she was dangling from the light fittings it

An excellent example of a former Metropolitan Police
'Panda' car now on display at the Dover Transport Museum
(https://www.dovertransportmuseum.org.uk) and reproduced with
their consent. Copyright of the museum is gratefully acknowledged.

Local goods transport available for hire

Kauda village in the Nuba Mountains. Local HQ of the SPLA

Chief of Staff, Col. George McGarr, with a Martini Henry rifle, potentially from the 1898 Battle of Omdurman

Cattle herders on the road to Kadugli. A real man always carries a weapon

JMC Mi8 helicopter

GoS Police outside their station in the Mirri Hills

Incoming sandstorm at Khartoum

Overwhelmed by the storm and world turns red

Hell's Gate Park and cooperative of zebras and a giraffe

Cannon on the beach at Timor Leste

The emblems of the red cross, red crescent, red crystal, and red lion and sun are symbols of neutrality and protection used during armed conflicts, and their use is restricted by law. The author wishes to thank the United Kingdom Ministry of Defence and the British Red Cross Society for authorisation to use these emblems in this book.

was easy to be unaware of her until she screeched. Apart from Zoltan's languages, Polly was also understandable in Spanish. Like all talking birds she had a wide vocabulary of obscenities but her favourite was in response to the office front-door bell when she would shout out "Closed. Come tomorrow" in rather nasal English or *"Poshel von!"* (Go away!) in Russian. Polly lived on a constant supply of nuts, which she shelled leaving the debris over the floor, fruit and crackers which she would steal from desks but her main source of protein was the fingers of anyone silly enough to try to tickle her under the chin.

Zoltan had arranged my Osijek Hotel booking and was concerned that it would be acceptable until I'd found an apartment. They had only squeezed me in because he'd told them I was a very important British diplomat but were otherwise very fully booked with the Croatian State Basketball Team. I felt a lot better; perhaps I wouldn't be spending all my time avoiding neck-ache. I took over contacts with the police in our area then expanded to deal with political and economic matters as I became more familiar with the local personalities. Zoltan left the OSCE a few months later and returned to Bulgaria while I took over as HFO in Osijek. The last I heard of Zoltan he was his country's ambassador elsewhere in Europe; I wish him well wherever he is.

*

Sometime later, flying home from Zagreb to Heathrow for a couple of weeks' leave, I came across a magazine article left in the seat pocket by a previous passenger. It was a very colourful travel piece about the interesting and ancient cultures along the Adriatic coast. The writer described the wine, the food and scenery and obviously knew the people well and had enjoyed living among them. His only regret was that although they warmly welcomed strangers they constantly fought bloody wars between themselves. The article was mainly taken from the writings of a Roman general 2,000 years before but nothing much had changed – and probably still hasn't.

Serbs, Croats and Bosnians, to name but three of the better known ethnic groups in the region, can still be relied upon to take up cudgels (swords, axes, daggers, grenades, AK47s, RPGs) on a point of honour or the drop of a perceived insult. Not long after I arrived a rather cynical, but probably quite correct, diplomat told me he had a theory that if you put any five Balkan men together they'd form nine political parties. The ladies showed much better sense and were usually the most significant calming influence in preventing bloodshed.

*

'Honour' was not simply an abstract concept but a guiding principle of life – and often death. Closely linked to honour was the notion of 'manliness'; how a real man should present himself to the world, conduct his affairs and live his life. Foremost among these qualities was the consumption of large volumes of ardent spirits. My home-made cider will anaesthetise your fingertips and make you wonder why your knees no longer work the way they did this morning but, in the Balkans, almost every village has two or three old ladies who specialise in making whatever the local preference demands and the neighbourhood fruit production will allow. The best known is probably *slivovitz* or plum brandy (from Croatian and Serbian '*sliva*' meaning 'plum'). Just about everything else, whatever fruit it may be based on, is usually referred to as *rakia* (*rakya, rakija, ракия*). If you look up recipes for these you can find several but what they seem to have in common is that the base spirit is usually vodka plus a range of flavourings. This is because in most countries it is highly illegal to distil ethanol spirit from fermented fruit juice. Fermentation is okay – my cider might give you a headache but it won't be an illegal one – but distillation will result in a visit from those nice chaps from Customs and Excise and a long relaxing break in one of Her Majesty's holiday homes. Attitudes vary, however, and in some parts of the Balkans it's okay to brew up just for private consumption. In the area where I worked that was interpreted as not more than ten litres per year per adult registered as living at a specific address. Well, that's all right then, just ten bottles per year, eh? But ten litres is over two gallons.

I was introduced to Olga, an elderly Croatian lady and the mother of a member of our local staff, who lived alone but in a house where six other adults were registered as being resident. In fact, three lived in Canada and two had moved away years before to another village. This charming pensioner was producing *rakia* on an almost industrial scale but never had more than twelve gallons on the premises at any given moment. Who knew, eh? Actually, just about everyone knew but she was tolerated because she made the best moonshine in the district. When I was taken to Olga's home she immediately dashed to her neighbour's house to bring in her friend to chaperone our meeting. What would people say if she, at a mere seventy-five, should be seen to be entertaining a male visitor? I was next told, not asked, that I would have a meal and a large dish of huge pasta dumplings was prepared. It was as I was eating this, it would have been impossibly insulting to refuse, I was given a beer glass of what I thought at first was plain water. Wrong. It was about half a pint of her *rakia* and I knew that I had to drink it on pain of not being regarded as a real man and losing face. I calculated that if I could get it straight down, the heavy pasta would slow it long enough for me to have about three quarters of an hour to drive back to my flat while I still had a reasonably well-functioning brain. Tomorrow was Saturday so I could afford an extra couple of hours in bed as the office was closed. The only downside to this plan was that my route home was largely cross-country and while not 'off-road', the roads were narrow and twisted and ran through an area not yet declared landmine free. The tarmac was safe enough but it was a very good idea to stay off the grassy verges; I still remembered the government public information films of my childhood.

Well, I'm writing this so you will have guessed I made it okay. No incident at all on the way home before I parked and went to bed.

At about eight o'clock the next morning I awoke, remarkably clear-headed, to the sound of Stepan, my landlord, tapping on my kitchen window. I had a first-floor flat and he had climbed to the balcony to reach the kitchen. He apologised from the depth of his being that he had to bother me on my day off but would I please come and move my car so his wife could get out. I smiled and, of course, said I would come immediately but privately thought that she should be able to get out of a parking space. And why had he climbed to the balcony anyway?

I had been driving a large Nissan Patrol 4x4 and parking the previous night had been a matter of simply driving front-end first into the bay outside the house but now I could see the lady's dilemma. My front bumper was almost touching the front door and doors here opened outwards. Stepan had climbed out of his bathroom window, then up to my balcony to wake me so that she, poor lady, could be released from their flat. To make matters worse I had managed to run the Nissan along the flower beds on either side of the path to the front door and would have to do so again as I reversed out. I spent the rest of the morning finding a jobbing gardener to repair the damage – to the delight of my landlady who was left with the best garden in the street.

*

A regular part of my role was to meet with the mayors and representatives of towns and villages in my area. Usually the meetings were cordial but quite formal and I even wore a tie! Invariably meetings started at about 7.30am with extremely strong coffee served with *slivovitz* or *rakia*. Quite by accident I found a way of avoiding this without losing face. I had been prescribed a short course of antibiotics for something not too dire but I was warned not to mix them with alcohol. Had I announced the death of a dear close relative the people I met could not have been more shocked or sympathetic. They drank to my health but didn't press me to join them. That course of antibiotics saw me through two years in the Balkans and later into Central Asia (where alcohol and the Islamic culture seemed to merge without conflict).

The mission channelled funds into towns and villages for rebuilding and development but avoiding loss through old-fashioned corruption was a serious concern. The mayor of one small town went to great lengths to avoid meeting me during a period when I was pressing him to show me what he had done with a significant financial grant arranged by my predecessor. The buildings he'd mentioned in the application had not been refurbished but he was, reportedly, driving a rather nice new BMW. My first request for a meeting resulted in a phone call from his secretary the day before to cancel and arrange a new date. That's okay, it happens. On the new date he was called away unexpectedly and his secretary could not say when he would be back. It turned out to be two weeks and this pattern carried on for another six. His Worship, like most local men, liked to get to the office about 7.30am so on the day of my next appointment I arrived at 6.30. I would usually drive myself but on this day I had the office driver with me. We parked across the square until I saw the BMW arrive and the mayor had gone in. My driver moved our car to park immediately under the mayor's second-floor office window while my interpreter and I went up to the mayor's secretary. She was so sorry but the mayor had been called away and she didn't expect him back for several hours. I explained that having come this far I was quite happy to wait.

In fact, we'd given him just enough time for his first couple of cups of coffee and half a bottle of brandy when we settled down outside his office door and it was really just a matter of my patience versus his capacity for holding liquid in the morning. It was a bit of an unequal challenge as he was doubtless suffering from the same problems that afflict many of us chaps in middle age. His secretary fielded three or four telephone calls, probably including from himself, and apologised profusely for wasting my time. Would I like to reschedule? Would I like to go into the town and have lunch? But miracles do happen and at eleven thirty, four hours into his day, he emerged from his office to the amazement of his secretary, but not my driver who later told me he had waved and said "Good morning" as His Worship started to climb out of the office window at about eleven o'clock. Meetings with civic officials hadn't been this much fun since the seventies on the fraud squad.

*

Osijek, unlike Vukovar, lacked obvious signs of recent fighting, but there remained a great deal of animosity between Croats who felt that they had been treated badly by Serbs over the generations. During the war many Serbs had abandoned their homes, mainly farms, and fled to Serbia. Now the war was over some were beginning to trickle back and often found their houses had been blown up, burned out or simply occupied by people who refused to leave. Getting redress through the courts was, at best, problematic. During the war a new car belonging to a Serb resident in a predominantly Croat village had been commandeered for 'official' use. Five years later he asked for his car back but was eventually forced to take his claim for compensation to court. The court issued an order for the return of the now badly damaged vehicle but ordered the owner to reimburse the village authorities for the costs of maintenance during the three years after it had been seized.

Everywhere in the Balkans firearms were a common feature of life. Almost without exception, men had experience of handling and using weapons from pistols to rifles, machine guns to rocket launchers. Owning a firearm was part of being a 'man' and there was a thriving market in most things that go bang including hand grenades, rockets and even landmines. While legal regulations did exist in theory, they were not stringent and, in practice, were largely ignored. The US Ambassador brought in some very significant funding to 'buy' weapons in private hands and a flat rate was paid to anyone handing over a weapon regardless of age, type or condition.

The programme ran for a few months until several tons of firearms of different types had been accumulated.

In similar programmes elsewhere the surrendered weapons were usually crushed under road rollers, chopped up by guillotines or dumped in the deep ocean but ours were to be recycled in grand style. Just south of Zagreb, in the city of Sisak, was a steelworks capable of producing hundreds of tons of liquid steel. Truckloads of weapons were brought in under police escort and loaded into hoppers then dropped into the mouth of the furnace. The whole event was televised which will always attract local VIPs, politicians and people famous for being famous. I had never seen metal in molten form and was expecting something like glowing plasticine but when I was handed a welder's mask to see inside it looked like boiling milk. I asked why things like wooden rifle stocks or plastic grips had not been removed but it seems they simply vaporised and were blown away in the first seconds. All this took place in front of TV crews and reporters declaiming the arrival of peace at last. Four liquid metal samples were drawn off and cooled. One went to the laboratory to be tested for purity, another was given to the US Ambassador for putting up the money and a third became a souvenir for the programme director. The last one is sitting on my desk now as a half-kilo paperweight.

Later that year I met the officer in charge of border crossings into Hungary in the north-east who told me that during the period of the buy-back programme a brisk trade developed importing old, rusted and completely useless WWII German Army rifles and pistols to surrender, no questions asked.

*

Part of the remit of the OSCE was the monitoring of elections, led by a team brought in for the purpose, under the Office for Democratic Institutions and Human Rights always known simply by the acronym ODIHR; unfortunately, it's pronounced 'Oh dear' which always felt very negative. Election monitoring is a labour-intensive job and most of the mission's expat personnel were pressed into service to help out. The national elections in January 2000 were widely predicted to bring a huge swing away from the incumbent party of government, the HDZ, 'The Croatian Democratic Union' (*Hrvatska demokratska zajednic*, literally Croatian Democratic Community), a centre-right party which had been in power since 1990, before the break-up of Yugoslavia. It has since returned to power in coalitions with centre-left parties.

On the day of the election in 2000 I had four polling stations to look after. At the first one the supervisor proudly showed me his ballot boxes. These had come flat-packed to be assembled on site then tied around with string and sealed with red sealing wax. His boxes were covered in seals, most impressive, but there was no bottom in any of them and the ballots just fell through. "No problem," he said and promised to ensure that they were all picked up before he closed. Another polling station was in a village with a large Islamic community where the polling station was located in a musty bar. Sullen-looking men in black leather jackets stared at anyone coming in, including me and, not surprisingly, many voters, especially women, were reluctant to enter. The bar owner, who was also the polling station supervisor, didn't seem to regard it as a problem, nor the enormous party banner across the outside of the building. Turnout in that village was low.

*

From Osijek it was possible to drive across the border into Hungary at Udvar. The CD plate on the car and a diplomatic ID made the crossing easy and it was better to go shopping at Tesco in Pécs than local shops in Osijek where only one kind of anything was available, if at all, and prices were still high. With a couple of days to spare it was possible to get as far as Budapest, a seriously nice city where the Hotel Gellert still operated to opulent 1920s' standards and the rate of exchange of the Forint made you feel very wealthy. OSCE vehicles could be used privately at weekends but availability was not guaranteed and when I found János, a Volkswagen dealer in Hungary who also hired cars, I became a regular customer. Arriving at his showroom to collect my VW Passat one Saturday morning he was deeply sorry to have to tell me it was still being serviced but I could have my choice of two other cars he had available. One was a black Mercedes limousine with extra dark tinted windows all round, including the windscreen. It was also armour-plated and weighed about four tons. Fuel was cheap but this thing probably only did about 5mpg. János said it was very popular with some of his business customers from Russia.

The other was a Trabant, that glittering gem in the crown of the old German Democratic Republic people's motor industry. It had a wooden frame under a body made of something like resin on glass fibre mesh which, I was told, gave off a toxic gas if it caught fire. There were tiny drum brakes on all wheels and the transverse mounted engine had a gravity-fed five-gallon petrol tank mounted above the exhaust manifold. In a front-end collision, if the crash or ensuing fire didn't get you, the fumes would. I went to a cafe and waited until my VW was ready.

*

I take the view that the new millennium began on 1st January 2001 but in late December 1999 the world was being told to expect that the failure of all computer systems with the year 2000 would cause aeroplanes to fall out of the sky, nuclear power stations to go into meltdown and, generally, world-wide apocalypse and the End of Days. In preparation, most Croatians arranged a party and I saw in the New Year with several local friends at a fireworks party around a bonfire on the roof of an apartment block in Osijek.

A couple of months later a vacancy arose at Mission HQ in Zagreb and I moved there to take over as the ambassador's policing affairs advisor. (Like the title? I thought of that. Until then it had been police advisor (PA) but caused a bit of confusion with personal assistant (PA), policy advisor (PA), political advisor (PA) and press advisor (PA). Acronyms can be so helpful.)

My new job allowed me to get around parts of the country I hadn't seen before and I even got back to Kraljevica, on the northern Adriatic Coast where I'd been on holiday over a quarter of a century earlier. It hadn't changed greatly as the worst effects of war had not been felt there. But now being located in Zagreb, and a member of the OSCE Ambassador's staff, I had to go to Vienna from time to time for meetings which meant driving myself. The road was not too good until the Austrian border when it became a typical autobahn with rest areas which were almost tourist resorts in themselves. It was usual to send a memo round to other departments so that anyone else wanting to go along could make use of the opportunity to use a single vehicle for the journey. The trip was something over 250 miles and took the better part of a day but some expats boasted of doing it in about four hours door-to-door. We even had a Swedish expat in Zagreb, who'd bought a duty-free Jaguar and boasted that he could get home to Sweden on a Friday night and be back in the office in time for the group meeting with the boss on Monday morning.

Zagreb was almost untouched by the conflict and most of the damage had been repaired before I arrived. The government was keen to be seen to be cooperating with anyone or any organisation which would polish its international image enough to get in to the EU. I made some helpful contacts such as the Deputy Minister of Interior, the de facto head of police, and although I'm sure he wasn't the only senior government officer to carry a pistol, he was the only one I met who kept it handy on his desk.

The UN mandate to run policing in Bosnia was coming to its end in 2002, by which time I had been in the Balkans for more than three years, so when discussions began about whether the OSCE or the EU Policing Unit would assume responsibility I made it known that, either way, I would be interested in moving to Sarajevo. In the end the job was given to the EU and I was offered a place on the planning team in Brussels with a view to going to BiH at the take-over. But that's another story for another time. Suffice to say that I didn't stay in Brussels long enough to draw my first month's salary and went home for a long break until a phone call one day inviting me to go to Africa.

IX

———

Here be Dragons

Africa

Everyone should take time to live, work and travel in Africa. The continent has been criss-crossed by explorers and plundered by invaders ranging from small gangs of pirates to the armies of most of the countries of Europe and Asia since long before the Northern Arabs, Romans and Greeks saw it as a source of riches and slaves. It's not possible to be in Africa for just a few years and say that you know it. Somewhere that vast can't be absorbed in just one lifetime, much less three or four years. Even today it's difficult and often quite dangerous to get around; Google Earth is probably no more help today in showing what's actually happening on the ground as those early maps with a mysteriously vague interior marked *Here be Dragons*. But I love Africa. How can you not be impressed by a whole continent spreading across the world ranging from sandy desert to tropical forest and from freezing mountain tops to plains hot enough to melt the rubber seal around your car windscreen? The people I met were mostly friendly, although there were exceptions of course, and most village people just wanted to live a modest life in peace while most of their leaders just wanted to live an immodest life of luxury and power.

Tribalism is often regarded by outsiders as being indicative of a primitive culture but that couldn't be further from the truth. 'Tribe' is important to many African people in a way that outsiders can't comprehend, the nearest equivalent possibly being the kind of clan loyalty still found in Eastern Europe. It means much more than just family, although very often it's the same as 'family', and binds people more strongly than simply the name of the country on their passport. National boundaries come and go, and most of them were imposed by outsiders anyway, but 'tribe' is constant. It took me a couple of years to really appreciate the hold that tribal loyalty has over individuals and I can think of no better illustration than a conversation with a taxi driver in New York.

I was on my way to the airport after a week in the city and got a classic yellow cab driven by a black New Yorker of about thirty-five. While we were stuck in traffic he asked where I was from and I told him 'London'. He said he wanted to visit London but would have to save up for a long while yet. I asked where he was from and he said he'd been born in Sudan but had come to the USA when he was about fourteen. I asked where he was from exactly and he said it was a little place called Julud that no one had ever heard of but, in fact, I knew it very well and wanted to show off a bit. Had he been to the village school built by Colonel Gadhafi or the Catholic school? Had his family been involved in the fighting? Would he ever go back? Then I asked, "And what tribe are you?" We had reached the JFK drop-off by now and my driver, whose name, he told me, was Abdullah, was almost in tears. In over twenty years in the USA, and ten years driving a taxi, I was the first person who'd actually known the place where he came from but, more importantly, I'd asked him about his tribe. I told Abdullah I was going back to Sudan, and would probably go to Julud soon, so I would pass on his greetings. About three weeks later I met the chief of his tribe and mentioned my New York cabbie.

The chief said their mothers were distant cousins and told me the name of the lady who'd gone to America and about Abdullah. He was still a son of the tribe and always would be.

*

My first experience of Africa had been in Ghana in 1996 following a murder in London. After a lot of political persuasion we had been given permission to go to a village in the north which meant we had to fly to Accra then travel north through the regional capital of Kumasi accompanied by police. There was a long two-day drive through forests of tall trees with root systems like the flying buttresses of mediaeval cathedrals. Most of the road was pretty good but then it would simply disappear for a couple of miles and reappear later. In West Africa, in rural Ghana, a 'white man' was '*Bruni*'. But this was far from a friendly greeting; *Bruni* were men who had been killed by demons who drank their blood making the bodies turn white before bringing them back to life to use as slaves. Given that many real slaves from West Africa ended up in the Caribbean, the similarity with the West Indian zombie legend can't be a coincidence. I remember seeing a child aged about three in northern Ghana staring at me in frozen, open-mouthed terror. Just then I was joined by my colleague who had very fair skin, white-blonde hair and pale blue eyes. That was too much for this poor kid who just turned and ran. I'm sure the next time his mum told him to behave or 'the Bruni will get you' he did as he was told.

In Sudan the equivalent term was '*Hawajah*' and much later a local interpreter had explained that *Hawajah* was probably bush Arabic/Swahili or, he said, it might have been Greek, or maybe neither. I think, perhaps, he felt embarrassed to say he didn't really know. It meant 'stranger' or 'traveller' and given the area's long history as a source of supply to the slave trade over hundreds of years the Arabic or Greek root might have some validity. There was a long tradition of welcoming outsiders and the term was used as a respectful and friendly term of address although, for all practical purposes, it was synonymous with 'white man'. Children would come out in mobs when we passed through villages waving and shouting "*Hawajah, Hawajah*" which sounded like "How are ya? How are ya?"; very different from the '*Bruni*' which had followed us around in West Africa.

*

After that first visit to Ghana it was to be about eight years before I would be able to go back to Africa to work in Sudan. I now described myself as an itinerant labourer for the FCO although later I would call myself a 'consultant'. Not only because it sounded more impressive but it was also easier to hire a car at Heathrow as a 'consultant' even though it usually meant being addressed as 'Doctor'. My introduction to the expat life in Kosovo, Croatia and the EU Police Unit in Brussels had followed a more or less similar pattern but the telephone call to go to Africa started differently. I had been having some very informal conversations with my friend Julius at the FCO about joining an observer team in Ramallah, north of Jerusalem, where, apparently, there had been a bit of friction between the Palestinians and the Israelis (for about the last 2,000 years) and I was expecting a call to get details of dates and flights. Instead Julius asked if I was aware of what was happening in Sudan. I was – not too big a fib. The FCO had been asked to find a policing specialist to join a military mission in somewhere called the Nuba Mountains and he wondered if I would be interested? I was. The packing kit-list would be mostly the same – allow for hot and sandy and lots of flies – so preparation just entailed sending my passport to the FCO to get a visa, buying three months' supply of anti-malaria tablets, my signature on the contract and off I could go. What he didn't say was that, in all probability, no UK police force wanted to risk losing a serving senior officer for months (or, as it turned out, years) while unskilled labourers like me were both cheap and expendable.

Because it was a long way off, and the news media tend to have the attention span of a mollusc, more than twenty years of civil war had been largely ignored by the West. Two million people were dead and while the northern part of the country remained firmly under government control things became problematic further south. The media tended to oversimplify the conflict as being a war between the Islamic north against the Christian south or the Arab north against the Black African south while in fact it was very much more complex. On each side there were several factions with competing interests: mixtures of racial, ethnic and religious factors representing all the various peoples and faiths in Sudan from Christianity to Islam as well as some very much older than either. Significant external political interests were vying with economic and developmental factors pulling in different directions.

Sudan

2002

On 1st January 1956 an agreement, signed two years earlier in 1954, between France and Great Britain took effect and 'The Republic of the Sudan' had become fully independent. Sudan used to be the largest country in Africa, almost the size of Western Europe, until the creation of South Sudan which divided the country across an east/west line in 2011 in accordance with the terms of a referendum held under the terms of the Comprehensive Peace Agreement of 2005. Although the country had been governed by its own parliament for many years, laws and legal procedures had, for the most part, been lifted originally almost unchanged from the UK but over the years, influenced most strongly by Islamic sharia law, adaptations had come about and, eventually, offences such as theft, murder, blasphemy and 'adultery' (covering most sexual immorality, indecency and impropriety) were criminal matters for which sharia-type punishments were prescribed under the various sections of the criminal code.

The system of policing was still in the British colonial pattern developed in India and modelled on the British Army of the nineteenth century, replicating ranks and discipline. Policing in areas under the control of the Government of Sudan (GoS) was provided by the official national police force controlled from their HQ in Khartoum to which the various regional HQs were subordinate. Police fell under the Minister of Interior but was completely military in structure and training. Officers were drawn from the upper levels of society and trained centrally in Khartoum. Lower ranks were recruited and trained regionally. Discipline was draconian; orders were followed without question and professional standards were poor. Training included firearms and military skills but it was not a requirement that lower rank recruits should be able to read and write. Police were held in low public esteem – there was not even a word, such as 'constable' for the lowest rank of police who were simply referred to as 'soldiers'. Accommodation was provided as well as supplies of food and medical facilities, including for wives and children, but pay was still so low that, inevitably, other ways to augment income were often found.

In the southern half of the country the Sudan People's Liberation Movement, the SPLM, and its military wing, the Sudan People's Liberation Army, the SPLA, were the principal actors in the armed insurrection against the official government of Sudan. By the time I arrived in 2002 the SPLM had established a de facto system of administration, including a police force which was comprised mostly of SPLA fighters some of whom had once been members of the GoS police, under a chief of police who had formerly been a GoS police colonel before going over to the rebel side.

One of the most difficult hurdles to get over had been who should be invited to take part in peace negotiations. The government of Sudan would obviously represent the official side but at different times, in various areas, there had been the usual alphabet soup of acronyms of competing forces and political groupings some of which spent most of their time fighting each other. The problem was finally resolved in a meeting in the Nuba Mountains region of Southern Kordofan in the central highlands. The location chosen was Kauda, deep within rebel territory where the 'Kauda Conference' and the subsequent Machakos Protocol resulted in the various factions being able to go forward under the flag of a single leader – John Garang, always known as 'Doctor John' – and the Sudan People's Liberation Movement. The military wing, the Sudan People's Liberation Army, even absorbed some of the smaller fighting forces.

The GoS now had a clear negotiating partner and it was possible to begin talks under the chairmanship of a Kenyan army general, Elijah Sumbeiywo, in Nairobi and later at Naivasha in the Rift Valley, which led to the Comprehensive Peace Agreement three years later. The other main outcome was the Nuba Mountains Ceasefire Agreement which allowed people in Southern Kordofan to resume a more or less normal way of life in an area which had seen some of the worst fighting and abuse of the population and showed what a 'normal' life could be like if the fighting stopped; many fighters had been born into the conflict and had never known peace. Both sides agreed to end operations, and withdraw their forces across an area about the size of Austria and a monitoring mission, the Joint Military Commission (JMC) was put in place to oversee compliance. The JMC was a small contingent of military and ex-military personnel sponsored diplomatically and financially by the UK, USA, Norway and Switzerland operating on the ground through the Joint Monitoring Mission (JMM) based in Kadugli, the regional capital of Southern Kordofan in the Nuba Mountains.

*

I joined the JMM on secondment from the FCO in 2002 and went to live in Kadugli where my role was to act as advisor on police affairs to the head of mission, a Norwegian army general, and oversee development of civil police forces of both sides. It was the beginning of the four very best years of my career living in a part of the world where, even now, few people from the outside have ever been. As part of the ceasefire monitoring process we undertook regular long-range patrols out into the bush and desert to meet and reassure people in remote areas, mediate in complaints of breaches of the terms of the agreement and discuss problems they might be having such as raids by cattle thieves or issues with the tribe over the hill not being prepared to share water. Most importantly the patrols raised our profile with very large white Toyota Buffalo 4x4s flying very large yellow flags. In the wet season the vehicles were useless so we used helicopters or even, sometimes, hired camels.

The quality of policing varied enormously from place to place but some incidents could have been transferred unchanged to the desk of any police officer anywhere as the same violent/dishonest/stupid people do the same violent/dishonest/stupid things to the same victims/spouses/casual acquaintances everywhere in the world.

I was invited to sit in on a training session at a regional training unit where 200 recruits were brought into a stiflingly hot and humid building with a corrugated steel roof which made it feel a bit like a tandoori oven. There was no electricity and, therefore, no lights or air conditioning, not even a fan. The four large windows and the door were wide open which allowed a very modest amount of air circulation. Long wooden benches provided somewhere for most to sit but a few had to stand at the back or sit on the floor. A police colonel stood at a lectern and read the text of the law relating to theft starting at page 1 through to page 200 while I followed on an English text and with the help of my interpreter. He did so uninterrupted pausing only to take a sip of water now and then. I'm old enough to remember the Larceny Act 1916 and recognised most of what he read out. Clearly, 'theft of wills' was still a major problem in bush villages as it received the same amount of time as theft from ships – 1,000 miles from Port Sudan. There were no questions. To ask a question would imply that the colonel had not read the text correctly, which would have been insulting, or that the questioner had not understood, which would have been an appalling admission. This was the only instruction on the subject these trainees would ever receive unless, if they could read at all, they studied in their own time.

*

Corruption was so deeply ingrained in the culture of the population that it was regarded as quite normal at all levels and while senior officials, on both sides, showed appropriate horror at any suggestion that such practices existed, we all knew the truth of the situation. A hospital in the area had been gifted a redundant ambulance by a town in the UK. I saw the vehicle for the first time shortly after I arrived when I found it sitting up on four piles of bricks with no wheels. A senior local official had a 4x4 with wheels and tyres of the same size but I'm sure this was purely coincidental and no untoward assumptions should be drawn.

On a drive through the bush a few weeks later I was flagged down by a policeman who politely told me that I had killed a chicken as I drove through a village some miles back although he had no vehicle or radio and it wasn't clear how he could have known about it. His point was that the family who owned the chicken should be compensated. I said that I did not believe I had hurt any chicken but asked, out of curiosity, what such a chicken might be worth. The officer told me that it had been a fine example and almost a family pet of the children who were very upset but $50 would ease all their grief. We discussed the life expectancy and value of local poultry for about a quarter of an hour and he eventually agreed that compensation of $2 would be adequate and he would, if I wished, undertake to negotiate with the family himself but I needed to leave him the money immediately. I was most grateful for his help but didn't tell him that I would have paid $5 just for the entertainment value of the negotiations. These examples might seem trivial or even amusing but when corruption is seen as normal at the bottom end, it persists easily and is accepted without question all the way to the top.

*

As with the KVM, part of the role of the JMM was to maintain as high a profile as possible and be seen travelling in the region to emphasise that it was safe to do so. Roads consisted of tracks and were useable by our vehicles only in the dry season when we could look forward to days of off-road driving and overnight camping – and, yes, I was paid to do this! (When camping in the jungle always use a hammock but dip the suspension cords in the diesel fuel tank to deter creepy crawlies, snakes, rodents or anything else from coming along them to join you in your sleeping bag during the night. Happy Camping!) When the rains began, we had to use our helicopters and a couple of Antonov light aircraft. I was allocated my very own Toyota Landcruiser which I proceeded to almost destroy over the next two years.

To comply with the terms of the ceasefire agreement we took an observer from both sides with us wherever we went. In my case I had a GoS police captain, Akram, and a SPLM police lieutenant, Ibrahim, allocated to my team as well as the interpreter. On a long drive out through the bush and grassland one day Lieutenant Ibrahim remarked that his home village was just beyond a hill to our right. It wasn't on our itinerary for the trip but these things were always flexible so we took a detour. We arrived in a bush village which looked deserted but that was quite normal as everyone was out working in the fields while the children looked after the goats. In the centre of every village there was always a structure called a 'rakuba', a very simple thatched shelter with no walls where village meetings were held, so we just sat in the shade and waited. After about ten minutes a child came out and gave us a jug of water, a traditional gesture of welcome to visitors. Ibrahim spoke to the boy and he went away. Nothing happened for another half an hour then bedlam erupted. The village filled with children and their goats, women of all ages and old men – the young men were either off fighting with the rebel forces or had been killed. Ibrahim had gone away to fight with the SPLA six years earlier; he had not been home since and to the villagers it was as if he had been returned from the dead. No more work would be done that day. A goat was killed and turned into a BBQ in record time and several women insisted on washing my hands to thank me for bringing their son home. Ibrahim found his wife and children, two of whom were under four years old, and local tradition held that the children were his if he chose to accept them. If he rejected them he was free to do so and they and their mother would simply leave the village for ever, but he didn't and I cannot imagine a happier father meeting his family after years away.

GoS law did not apply in the ceasefire zone, or at any rate was not enforceable, and the prohibition on alcohol was one of the first things to be forgotten. The local beer or 'wine' was made from sorghum which is similar to maize and while it tended to look a bit like well-used dishwater with a thick yellow foam on top it actually tasted quite good if rather yeasty and, depending on the skill of the brewer, could have the effect of a DIY lobotomy. The celebrations were obviously going on for a long time but I had other visits to make before dark. The call of duty thus saved me from a drilling headache the next day and, with the rest of the team, departed leaving Ibrahim behind getting to know his new family and arranged to come back a week later.

*

Jane Austen remarked, *It is a truth universally acknowledged, that a man in possession of a good fortune must be in want of a wife.* I doubt whether she was thinking of nomadic tribes of cattle herders in the African bush but the principle still applies to what happened in a very small village just south of El Obeid. Even calling the place a village was a bit pretentious as it was really just a seasonal grazing area for a tribe of nomadic cattle herders. Setting up camp outside a village always caused a bit of a stir. The kids – human and goat – just wanted to climb over the vehicles to find whatever there was to eat.

The adults – human and goat – stood back in more dignified style but were equally curious. Eventually they decided that they might be able to persuade us to stump up some money to build them something or drill a well or do any of the other useful things that we *Hawajahs* (strangers) were noted for.

When night fell – no dusk in the tropics; God just turns off the lights – we were presented with a very welcome gift. Two boys from the village, on the instructions of the Omda/chief/headman, came to our camp with a large iron pot filled with glowing charcoal saving us the trouble of attempting to make our own cooking fire and the embarrassment of failing to do so. We were being treated as honoured guests. A meeting with an Omda usually ended with a meal but this was not obligatory; all that was 'required' was to offer a traveller water to drink. If the offer was simply just one cup of dirty water between four of us, it was the chief's way of saying, "I must offer you water. Now take your water and go." The only possible response was to refuse the water but such occasions were rare in the extreme. In four years it happened to me, maybe, twice. The first meeting with a village Omda is rather like a first encounter between two Boy Scouts. Woggles are exchanged and arms full of badges compared item by item. I couldn't compete with the numbers of cattle and sheep and I was totally outclassed in the offspring section on both children (seven to two) and grandchildren (five to zero). But I scored enough points with 'age' to carry the contest. Years were revered in a quite extraordinary way earning me a level of respect equal to that of the chief himself and not just a free bus pass. Before we could get down to talking about serious matters there was a further preliminary ritual of polite but formal exchange of personal histories. I learned that my host had killed a lion! This was an amazingly courageous feat in an area where lions had not been seen for more than fifty years; perhaps he was older than he looked. But I had faced and slain many, many clay pigeons. Actually, I had a little trouble with an explanation of what a 'clay pigeon' was exactly and he might have got the idea that it was some sort of large, fierce, carnivorous flying beast native to Great Britain.

While I had a mere one wife, to his three, he was seriously impressed that under British law I could have as many as I wanted. The interpreter missed the bit about, "…but only one at a time". Talk of family took us to discussion of my children, Desdemona and Horatio Dogberry. Even though 'Admiral' is a word borrowed from Arabic, the concept of a 'navy' is difficult to explain to anyone who has never been more than twenty miles from where he was born and lives nearly five hundred miles from the coast. But being a soldier in a ship bestowed significant respect on Horatio and brought honour to me. Such a duty easily explained and excused his lack of wives and consequent offspring. Hopefully these things would be remedied in time *en sh'Allaha*. My host was deeply saddened, however, to hear that Desdemona had chosen to pursue her own career, indeed she had even chosen for herself what that career should be, leaving her mother and living many days' walk from home. How ashamed I must feel. How desolate her mother must be. No doubt, if Horatio or I had been at home we would not have permitted such reprehensible behaviour.

The chief was a wealthy man with three wives and over a thousand cattle and goats, one of which was tethered outside the hut unaware that she was soon to be given a starring role in the traditional BBQ of Welcome. He was also quick to spot an opportunity. Two of his sons were still without wives and another, the eldest, had only one wife so a possible vacancy still existed even with him. The way forward was obvious. I should bring Desdemona on my next visit and make my choice of his three sons as a husband for my daughter. We agreed that his youngest son was probably still not yet a potential bridegroom being just fourteen years old but the others, nineteen and twenty-three respectively, were serious contenders. He was even prepared to waive his expectation of a dowry and throw in 200 cattle to achieve such a prestigious match. I had the feeling I could have negotiated this higher quite easily. Sadly, we were unable to reach an understanding on the final details and no marriage was possible.

Some months later while on leave in the UK and having dinner with the family I recounted these discussions. Desdemona was not amused. While highly appreciative of my efforts on her behalf, she told me quite firmly that she would attend to such matters herself. Horatio didn't say anything but a little later quietly asked, "Were they good cattle, Dad?"

*

Maps of Sudan showed roads all over the country but outside the towns these were more the fruit of a vivid imagination than survey on the ground. In some cases it was likely that funds had been made available to build a road but after 'shrinkage' of the budget there was not enough left to make it worthwhile even to start. The maps really only suggested where traditional migration routes and slaving routes had once passed through. In the wet season the actual location of a road might vary by anything up to four or five miles from where it was supposed to be. Levelling and clearing defined paths allowed villages to communicate and trade and was probably one of the most important projects the JMM undertook in the Nuba Mountains to build confidence that a lasting peace was possible.

The credit for the road building goes entirely to one man, namely my old friend from Kosovo Frank Seacole. He turned up in the mission one day wearing his signature floppy straw hat and got down to getting a broken-down grading machine working. For those of you unfamiliar with African rural highway construction, a grading machine looked rather like a classic drag racing car. It had a very long, extended chassis supported at the front by two small wheels and a huge tractor engine and wheels at the rear end. Roughly across the centre was mounted a large blade rather like a bulldozer with various hydraulic and pneumatic gadgets to raise and lower the blade and steer the machine. Frank would go off on his grader, sometimes for days at a time, often alone or with just one other local man to assist as interpreter, drive the 4x4 carrying food, fuel and a few spare parts, and generally help out. But it was Frank who was the magician of the machine. His roads were not surfaced and had to be touched up a bit after the rains stopped. They hardly qualified as motorways but often they were the first roads that had ever existed in these areas. I would guess that in two years Frank single-handedly levelled hundreds of miles of roads and I think of him every time I bump over the potholes in my village. (Devon Highways, please note.)

*

Over Christmas and New Year, the JMM base camp at Kadugli ran at minimum capacity for a few weeks. In my first year I wasn't due to go on leave until the new year and Christmas was a very strange time in camp for those of us left behind to mind the shop. Local people followed various faiths, some of them very much older than Islam or Christianity – they were, after all, the same people who had been building pyramids in Sudan before the Egyptians and while we were still submitting the planning application for Stonehenge. The predominantly Euro/American JMM personnel agreed by popular consent to observe 25th December as the day when we would do even less than we did for the rest of the holiday period. We had a quite well-stocked clubhouse and the camp kitchen produced the sort of food from a field kitchen which only army cooks can, i.e. extremely good and in huge quantity.

However, on Christmas Day I was very bored and had a week to while away before going home on leave. My own Landcruiser was in the workshop having a roof rack fitted to take the four spare wheels and extra jerrycans for fuel and water I had asked for, so when I decided to take a drive I took one of the Toyota Hi-Lux pickups. With so many expats on leave there was plenty of spare transport available and driving out of the camp was probably my favourite pastime – being paid to go off-roading in someone else's 4x4 where roads were just a notion or, if they existed at all, disappeared as soon as the rains came. Most of my colleagues preferred to fly but although helicopters were quick, convenient and great fun, no one actually lives up there and you don't convince people it's safe to travel if you don't set an example and do it yourself. Although, technically, not the dry season the ground had solidified to stone and my plan was to scout the route to a village on the other side of the *jebel*. *Jebel* is Arabic for 'mountain' and although we were always very polite and referred to them as mountains most were just hot, rocky hills; some even looked like oversized garden rockeries running alive with snakes and monkeys. There are higher *jebels* in Essex.

I was on my own but it was an easy drive and I simply needed to follow the dry goat tracks. After about an hour I met three women walking in the same direction. There was only one village in the area and we were obviously going to the same destination so when they flagged me down I was happy for them to climb up into the back of the pickup. Two were in their thirties and the third was a lady probably of about sixty-five who had clearly led a life of hard work in the sun. On their heads they were all carrying shallow circular baskets about three feet wide and heaped with grain which they wore like Ascot hats for the next hour while I bumped over the rutted track to the village. When we arrived the two younger ladies hopped off nimbly while I dropped the tailgate to help their older friend down. She handed me her basket as she did so but it was all I could do to hold on to it and nearly dropped everything on the ground which would not have pleased her at all. I certainly couldn't have lifted it up to head-height, much less balance it there to walk twenty miles in a sunny forty-five degrees, barefoot over rough ground.

*

I have enormous respect for 'tribal justice' as administered in some rural parts of the world but especially in Africa. The chief of a tribe was very often a blend of village constable, mayor and magistrate and dispensed justice according to local traditions going back beyond memory and simple common sense. Rules of evidence were whatever he decided them to be and decisions were the collective view of whoever turned up on the day to watch.

I remember this incident quite well; it's the subject of the only newspaper cutting I've ever kept. In February 2006, in a village in South Sudan, Mr 'A' was disturbed during the evening by strange noises coming from the compound behind his hut. Supported by several friends he went into the night and discovered Mr 'B' *in flagrante delicto* with a nanny goat owned by 'A'. (I might have said he was caught red-handed but that wouldn't be strictly accurate.) 'B' was secured and shamefully admitted that he had been overcome with passion for the young animal, whose name I will withhold. I suspect strong drink might also have played a part in the story – it usually does.

A committee of tribal elders decided that 'B' should not be handed over to police but would, instead, be required to pay a very substantial 'dowry' immediately and then the two should be married. Mr 'A' said, "We have given him the goat, and as far as we know, they are still together." As I write this the happy couple will be approaching their fifteenth anniversary. I hope they are still very happy.

X

———

Lizzie

One of the pleasures of working in rural Africa is being able to get out of the camp into the bush where driving off-road is irrelevant because, since the beginning of time, no one has ever bothered to build a road there. It's not just wise, but essential, never to travel alone – although I confess I did sometimes – and always have a rugged 4x4 with extra spare wheels on the roof and a winch to get out of trouble. On a journey to scout a new route between two villages my colleague Tybalt and I were sharing the driving in my Landcruiser. I have to say, he was the better off-road driver but even so we ended up using both of the spare tyres I had with me and there was no way to get back to the track we knew. We never saw any of the people living in the area but a very large dead vulture hanging upside down in a tree seemed to be the local equivalent of 'No Hawkers – No Circulars'. Going on took us into an area of sapling Acacia trees. Nothing else grew in the area; we couldn't go round it so there was no choice but to force our way through it. And that's how the bulky rounded sides of my Landcruiser became flattened.

In the wet season some areas were impassable except to camels and helicopters. Seeing a vehicle sitting up to its headlights in mud waiting to be pulled out was not uncommon. Later the ground would set like concrete covered in nine inches of dust and criss-crossed by a web of dry *wadis* which had been raging torrents just days before. The *wadis* could be as deep as they were wide and usually had steep, sandy, slippery sides.

On one such excursion I found my way ahead blocked where my track crossed a *wadi* about six feet deep with precipitous sides. The local equivalent of a Ford Transit was a cart welded together from an old truck axle and wheels and pulled by a donkey. In front of me a charcoal merchant had managed to load a bungalow-sized pile of sacks on his cart and had led his donkey into the *wadi* where it had stopped. The poor animal seemed to be saying to me, 'This idiot got me in here but only a miracle is going to get me out.' The owner had decided that whipping his animal from his seat on the shafts would provide the necessary motivation until I asked Mohammed, my interpreter, to explain that I would be happy to use the power winch to pull the cart out of the *wadi*. A miracle! *Shukran*! At first the driver thought I wanted him to attach the end of the cable to the bridle but this would not have helped at all. Removing the donkey from the shafts, we winched the loaded cart to the top. The grateful donkey driver insisted that he was now my servant for ever for helping him so I asked Mohammed to tell him that I was only helping the donkey and if I ever saw him whip a donkey again I would whip him. Everyone laughed and we continued on our way. Down the road I said to Mohammed, "You didn't translate that last bit, did you?" "No, Excellency," he said, "he would have thought you were a very silly man." Actually, I think Mohammed did as well.

*

Mohammed was a local man of about thirty-five and I enjoyed working with him enormously. He was from one of the wealthier families in the area, hence his education in Khartoum, and was a wonderfully reliable source of information on the traditions and customs of the region. He knew everyone and everyone seemed to know him which eased many introductions to what are now called 'influencers'. Mohammed had been brought up in a village near Kadugli at the bottom of a *jebel*. Thousands of years of weathering, extreme heat and cold nights, had covered the hills with amazing boulders and rock formations many of which looked highly precarious but must have been defying gravity for hundreds, if not thousands of years in some cases. When he was about ten years old he had gone up on the hillside with a couple of other boys looking for mischief. For about two weeks they spent every spare moment they had digging away at the base of a rock about ten feet high. It was immoveable and there wasn't the least sign of a wobble but they persevered. All they wanted to do was make it move a couple of feet, that's all, but when it did start it exceeded their wildest expectations. He told me that at first they started cheering but then realised it was going further than they had expected and there was no way to stop it. I have no idea what a ten-foot sphere of rock weighs but it must come in at over twenty tons and it was now rolling down a steep slope towards the road about a quarter of a mile away. Surely, it must slow down by then, mustn't it? The gradient was a bit less nearer the road but not enough to slow their oversized marble other than in their imagination. Just before the road there was a dry *wadi*. That's okay, that'll stop it – it didn't. The road was the main Kadugli to El Obeid route and one of the only hard-topped surfaces for miles around and usually quite busy. By some miracle their rock crossed the road between a bus going to El Obeid and a motorcyclist headed towards Kadugli. Now, all that was left was just a hundred yards of flat, level ground before the village itself. Their big bowling ball did indeed start to slow down but not enough. It was lucky to be a working day (so why weren't they at school?) and the village was largely empty. Anyone standing in front of their rolling rock would have been flattened like a cartoon character but luck was still with them and the only casualty was a donkey which wouldn't have known what hit it. By now it had almost run out of steam but made it to the middle of the village where it stood defying the boys to say it was nothing to do with them.

The next day, the Omda convened a meeting at which the elders, including the fathers of the three boys, discussed what punishment was appropriate. Accident? No. Allah had not had a hand in this. Unintended consequence of youthful exuberance? Perhaps but there was damage and there must be punishment. The outcome was that the three fathers must buy another donkey to replace the one killed. (The owner was delighted; it was an old animal anyway and just about any donkey still breathing would be an improvement.) The boys were all to be beaten by their fathers in view of the meeting; bad enough but the worst part was having to spend the whole of their school summer break, three months, looking after the village's entire herd of goats. That was a dawn-'til-dusk job, seven days a week. None of the boys complained but accepted what their fathers had decided.

Now working with the JMM, Mohammed was a learned man who commanded respect and whose days of rock rolling and dead donkeys were long in the past. One of the other boys involved had become an Imam while the third was in Khartoum as an instructor at the military academy. Life moved on and Mohammed's father announced that he had found him a wife with a good dowry from a village just outside Kadugli and would be honoured to have all the international JMM members come to the wedding. The ceasefire had allowed things like weddings to get back to pre-war style and as the joining of two important families this would be a major event. It had a lot in common with weddings in the Balkans where everyone seemed to bring an AK47 to joyfully fire thousands of rounds into the sky. After the first couple of days the happy couple were allowed to enter their house in the village which the groom's family had built for them. Over the door the bride's father had hung up a long camel whip and I asked why it was there. This, I was told, was a gift to the new son-in-law and a message from father to daughter that she now had a new master.

*

In the Nuba Mountains base camp in Kadugli, conditions were, to put it mildly, basic but after a while this just became the new norm. It was like travelling back in time technologically. We even stored data on floppy disks that lasted about a week because of the dust and humidity. (Readers under fifty will just have to ask a grown-up what a 'floppy disk' was.) There was an internet connection on dial-up but only if the phones were working. All our office furniture had been made in the camp and gave the whole place the look of that page in the Scouting Handbook showing all the things you could make in the woods. (Seriously, did anyone ever actually use a plate rack made from twigs? Whenever I was camping we didn't even wash plates between campsites let alone between meals.)

I got into the habit of covering my desk, chair and area of floor around them with a large cotton sheet at night. Sometimes there would be swarms of locusts and similar flying, hopping and squirming things which filled the room only to expire as soon as I turned on the air-conditioner to cool it down to a workable thirty-five degrees. They had to be cleared up before it was possible to sit down and usually filled a couple of large sacks which were dumped in the *wadi* to stink until one of the local staff was paid to dig a deep trench and bury them. They never did, of course, just scrapped a furrow and set fire to them with petrol.

Lifting the sheet in the morning was always done with some trepidation. Snakes and lizards could be an issue but the largest thing I ever found under my desk was a local youth practising for Young Burglar of the Year. He was no problem but scorpions had to be taken much more seriously and treated with respect. We had two kinds locally. The huge dark-brown/black ones lacked interpersonal skills but tended to be loners. They would stand their ground when disturbed and rear up aggressively mumbling, "Yeah – come on then if you think you're good enough." A sting from one of these was like the worst bee sting you can imagine accompanied by a burning swelling as if a large jalapeño chilli had been inserted under the skin. But they were easily swept off the table with a stick and clattered across the floor making a noise like my dad's false teeth. The real danger was from the others, the little yellow ones with a broad orange stripe from head to stinging tail. These always seemed to be in Millwall-supporter-sized groups and were about as friendly. Unfortunately, they were deadly and a single sting could be fatal. No matter how hot it was, I always kept my boots on – even in the shower.

*

The Soviet-designed Mi-8 (МИ-8) helicopter is a flying workhorse – a sort of aviation equivalent to a Ford Transit (other makes of utility commercial vehicles are available) and was the air transport equivalent of travelling in the back of a concrete mixer but not as comfortable, roomy or quiet. One of the most successful aircraft of its kind, about 15,000 have been built in different variants. (The Mi-28 is simply HUGE. It swallowed our fire engine whole without having to remove the ladders from the roof). I became used to them in Sudan both in my initial contract and later with the UN. Most were supplied on contract by Ukrainian companies which provided aircraft, pilots, crew and service facilities. Some of you may have used the helicopter service to the Scillies, or even flown in British military machines but ours were much more fun. Rotary wing vertical take-off works best in cold air so it's not as efficient in Africa. One of the pilots told me that in the oilfields in Siberia his aircraft could go straight up with five tons. In Sudan we could barely manage two tons with runway assistance and no more than one and a half vertically but only if you departed before 8am while the air was still cool. They are very noisy inside and a headset was essential to hold any kind of conversation with the person sitting next to you. The three-man crew (Women? Flying helicopters in Africa? Not quite ready for that yet) consisted of the pilot, co-pilot/engineer and loadmaster/gofer. The first two sat in proper seats on the flight-deck while the loadmaster used a piece of three-quarter-inch plywood between the front two seats once airborne. At take-off and landing the crew had to twiddle with controls in different parts of the aircraft including one at the rear of the cargo bay; this was obviously inconvenient and could probably have been designed out over the years but it did mean that if a crew member had been minded to defect he would have had to convince his two colleagues to go along with him.

Our flight regulations demanded that all passengers, crew and cargo had to be on board before the engines were started. There was no separate cargo hold and I spent many trips trying to keep goats from eating the sacks of grain across which I reclined. Inside was very hot indeed; air-conditioning and heating systems had been sacrificed to save weight and from closing the doors to getting airborne could take twenty minutes while the pilot tested the engines. Eventually the crews realised that we were grown-ups and could be trusted not to run around and would leave the main side door open until just before take-off – when the downdraft would have filled the inside with high speed, hot sand – and opening it again at altitude. It was a great way to travel, especially using a safety harness to sit on the edge of the door to take pictures. They wouldn't have let you do that going to the Scillies.

About nine months into my assignment in the Nuba Mountains the helicopter contract was given to a new company and all our friendly old Ukrainians were replaced with very dour new Ukrainians. One loadmaster insisted that everyone should be seated and strapped in, and goats tethered, with the doors closed before even starting the engines. He then gave the standard flight safety talk about emergency evacuation including use of life-jackets. This lasted for about a week until (a) the pilots found that their flight deck was as hot as our cargo bay and (b) use of life-jackets would probably not be an issue over the desert. Normal service was resumed.

*

Given the choice, I preferred to go out on my various trips overland in a Toyota 'Buffalo' 4x4 or by camel; it was all a matter of time

121

available. Riding a camel at about 4mph for three days out and three days back, with overnight camping and general Ripping Yarns-type adventures on the way, was certainly my preferred option. Sadly, I rarely had that much time available and an off-road trip of two or three days, taking in several outlying villages or tribal grazing areas was the norm except in the rainy season. If it was just too wet, or if I had a backlog of appointments, the only way was to fly.

In the better established settlements most of the buildings were brick-built (albeit of locally made and fired mud bricks) and usually had corrugated metal roofs. However, in rural areas buildings were usually thatched with whatever was growing locally. The nomadic cattle/goat/camel herders would put up quickly assembled circular shelters but generations ago had replaced skins with plastic sheeting scavenged from the UN World Food Programme or USAID.

We had set up a number of outlying stations housing a lone resident mission member and two or three local staff. These had to be visited regularly to rotate staff, resupply and generally deal with problems that might have arisen. If a suitable building wasn't available, we would build one (and leave it behind afterwards as a gift to the village). Construction was simple and planning consent consisted of a nod from the local Omda. One such sub-station was in a village in the north-east of our area where a river and traditional trade routes, formerly slave routes, crossed in the desert – west towards Darfur and south towards Juba, which would one day become the capital of South Sudan. Several tribes lived there in close proximity but not always in harmony and it was therefore essential to have a presence. Two or three older buildings, some more than a hundred years old, were generally solid but were surrounded by several dozen simpler houses of various designs made of thatch or light sheeting.

Generally, the mission got on well with local people. They knew why we were there and a prolonged ceasefire had even allowed markets to open up and thrive. For our part we respected their environment and lifestyle and interfered as little as possible. The police had even sent a lieutenant and half a dozen men to provide a 'presence' which seemed mainly to consist of sleeping under the trees and playing football.

I had arranged to have air transport to visit three of the more difficult to reach locations and just before take-off the HQ logistics officer asked me to include a visit to resupply the newest outstation. I hadn't met the new police commander so it all worked quite nicely. Landing in Devon in a large helicopter would certainly need permission and a police cordon to keep the curious from being crushed or decapitated but we tended to be more relaxed about these things in Africa. Normally we'd just make a low pass to announce our arrival as the pilot picked a suitable spot to put down. Unfortunately, it was the first time that this pilot had visited such a place. Low pass complete, we touched down safely and got out to be met by a very angry Omda, a distinctly unhappy police lieutenant and a furious Brit 'resident' mission member. Looking behind them I gathered the reason for their ire; our low pass, and touchdown had removed the thatched roofs, and most of the reed walls, from just about every building in the village. This was going to take more than a few handshakes and smiles to repair and the worst part was that after unloading we had to take off again and probably blow down anything we had left standing as we arrived. Some days it just didn't seem to come together.

*

After blowing down most of the huts in a neighbouring village with a helicopter (not my fault, I stress) my next trip to the area was a lot less dramatic. Two days' drive, with an overnight stop at a police station, took me to Julud, former home of my New York cab driver, a village in the north of our area where a number of tribes had lived in relative harmony for a very long time. We were not the only organisation present and there was very strong representation of all the international NGOs, religious and charitable groups which send well-intentioned, but often ill-prepared people to such places. Our local Julud base (JMM) was the largest and best resourced and tended to be the evening watering hole for most of the expat personnel for miles around. Between us we were also the largest employer in the region and contributed significantly to the local economy.

Before leaving on any long-range patrol it was normal to let other branches at the Kadugli HQ know about the route and timing so that best use could be made of the journey. This time I was accompanied by Anthony, one of our engineers, a Ghanaian with a wicked sense of humour and always good company. He had to visit our base to give the generator its monthly service and solve the mystery of why it seemed to have started using much more diesel than it should.

I got on with my appointments and didn't see my colleagues until late in the day. Anthony was a bit concerned about what he had found in the generator shed so the unit resident and I went out with him where he showed us several cables coming out of the switch box to connect to the offices and accommodation buildings. But another pair of cables went up the wall and over the roof and he had no idea what they were for. Next day we climbed onto the roof and followed the cables to where they went down and into the ground. This was too good to leave alone and gently pulling the cables Anthony was able to take them across the yard, under the gate and out to the street where they seemed to be buried a lot deeper. We left it until after dark, about 8pm, and then stood outside the gate while Anthony disconnected the cables from the generator. Instantly, about half the village was plunged into darkness including the premises of most of the local international teams.

We went back to our office and waited. After about ten minutes a crowd of local staff employed by our neighbours began to gather at our front gate looking for one of our security staff. This enterprising chap had previously been in the army and knew a little about generators; he had rigged up the extra line and was selling power to anyone in the village who would pay in cash. To be fair, most didn't know that the arrangement was unofficial but our small generator couldn't carry the load of the whole village and we had to stop supplying everyone except the local clinic and a couple of the more worthy recipients which we provided with electricity at no cost, pleasing them greatly. We also had a vacancy for a new security guard and saved a lot of fuel into the bargain.

*

At least as many journeys to outlying villages and tribes were conducted by vehicle, when the roads and weather allowed, as by helicopter, camel or walking. Stopping overnight and camping was an option but even when you could make the trip in a couple of hours it was still pleasant to pull over for a coffee sometimes. You could do this in the bush in Sudan as well and, to me, the product was much better than anything you'll ever have been offered in a smart chain where the choice of coffees alone is bewildering and it's necessary to undergo a five-minute consultation with a barista to make sure you know what you're going to get.

A roadside coffee stop in the bush in Sudan is a lot simpler although not necessarily quicker.

Ingredients:	Coffee beans (freshly picked, still white and unroasted)
	Water (as clean as may be had locally but without obvious signs of life)
	Sugar
	Ginger root to taste (optional)
Equipment	One 1955 British Army Bedford truck gearbox bell-housing and lay-shaft
	One 1955 British Army Bedford truck hubcap (front wheel)
	One 2 lb Heinz baked bean tin (or similar, empty and washed)
	Charcoal
Method	Squeeze the top of the baked bean tin to form a spout.

Using the charcoal, heat water to boiling and leave on the heat.

Place the hubcap (front wheel) on the charcoal and raise to a good heat. Add a generous handful of coffee beans and roast until dark brown, agitating constantly. Remove from the heat and put aside to cool.

When cool, place in the bell-housing and use the end of the gearbox lay-shaft to grind to an acceptable powder.

Put the ground coffee beans in the baked bean tin and add boiling water. Return to the heat and boil for five minutes. Add lots of sugar.

Shred some ginger root and use it to filter the ground coffee while pouring.

Serve and charge the customers whatever you think they will pay.

This was usually sold in a building about the size of the average garden shed made of wooden poles with woven walls and a thatched roof. The charcoal fire was inside in the middle of the floor but the doors and windows, just openings, allowed so much ventilation it never got more than moderately choking. The whole process usually took about ten minutes – or fifteen minutes if the water had to be boiled from cold or a new batch of beans roasted. There was a hard mud floor and we all sat around on logs. The coffee was the best I've ever had but although I have tried to copy the system in the UK, I can't get near it.

*

If you jet off on holiday to somewhere exotic you will, unless you are very silly (which your discerning choice of reading material clearly shows that you are not), make sure all your medical precautions have been attended to. I had previously been to West Africa at cost to the taxpayer (thanks again, taxpayer, I'm very grateful) and part of the preparation had been a pre-travel dose of mefloquine as a preventive measure against malaria. This was followed with one dose per week while in the affected region and several after return to the UK to ensure nothing unpleasant had come back with me. Going to Sudan there were similar considerations about disease but this time emphasised by the very basic living conditions. Mosquitos kill over 400,000 people in Africa every year, probably more than armed conflict, and I was keen not to add my name to either list of casualties but there was a problem with mefloquine taken over long periods. Just search online for side effects to see all the fun things that can happen ranging from mild confusion, through hallucinations, paranoia, psychosis and death not to mention potential for long-term liver and kidney damage. Having taken it before I knew that I was unlikely to react badly but I wasn't going for a three-week holiday; I would be in the country for years. I therefore made a conscious decision to take no prophylactic at all but to rely on a good mosquito net and accept the risk. On the plus side, although I was probably going to get malaria at some stage, by not using anti-malarial drugs it meant these would then be available as an effective treatment. The other side of that coin was that I was more likely to get malaria, but even when on regular mefloquine there was still a predictable probability of infection, and I was likely to be in the country long enough for that to become a reality. I did get malaria, but read on first.

The commonest side effects of a weekly anti-malaria dose are hallucinations which can range from somewhat exotic dreams to full-blown waking psychotic episodes. They are often terrifyingly real without ethereal dream-like qualities and colleagues who wake up screaming are not unknown. This is a bit of a nuisance when sharing accommodation with several other people. Working in an Islamic country we kept Friday as a rest day for our local employees. As expats we tended to take the same day off ourselves, or at least avoided leaving the camp. Having diplomatic status meant we had a bar which sold alcohol but only to internationals and was only open on Thursday evening, after close of business. Just about everyone, therefore, took their anti-malaria happy-tablet on Thursday before turning out the lights knowing they could sleep in the next day to get over it. As a non-user, there were several Thursday nights when I would lie awake listening to the frightened sobbing and jabbering of my colleagues despite being one the fortunate few in the camp with a private cabin.

Lizzie

Dengue Fever, also known as 'Break-bone fever', which I'm told is a pretty accurate description of how it feels – the clue is in the name – is carried by day-biting mosquitos. It wasn't a significant issue in our region but malaria, which is carried by a night-biting mosquito, was, and still is, a major cause of death throughout the region. Using a mosquito net, regularly steeped in pyrethrin, is very effective but it has to be set up properly and was not my only defensive tactic. Mosquitos are small and will get through the tiniest gap to inject a local anaesthetic and picnic on your blood quite painlessly while you sleep, unlike sand-flies which are small enough to get through the mesh of the mosquito net and are very painful indeed. In hot sunny places, and Sudan tends to be hot and sunny, there was a temptation to wear light clothes, shorts and T-shirts. I never did but always wore long-sleeved shirts, long trousers taken in to my boots at the ankle and a Drizabone Australian bush hat which I've had for over thirty years. It's been through tropical rain, blizzards and deserts. It's been packed in rucksacks, blown off clifftops and soaked in rivers. I know other makes are available and I just don't care. But, without any doubt, my best defence was Lizzie.

I found one day that a very large lizard had taken up residence under my bed. I'm not even sure how long she had been there before I noticed her, but coming back one evening after dark I switched on the light and caught her crossing the middle of the room (I assume female – her name was 'Lizzie' after all). She froze – *If I don't move you can't see me so I'm just going to stay very, very still.* This was one of the most beautiful animals I'd ever seen. She was about eighteen inches from nose to tail and had brilliant blue, orange and icy white markings. We looked at each other for about half a minute then she scampered under my bed when I took another step into the room. I looked under the bed with a torch but couldn't see her and assumed she had a private entrance through the wall. Several nights later I woke at about 3am and found her suspended on the mosquito net above my head. I let her stay but after that I always made sure the mozzy net was pulled taught and in good order. She spent the night patrolling the airspace over my bed for mosquitos and the day lurking under my bed looking for termites. I didn't get my first bout of malaria until after she had gone which is a sad tale in itself.

*

Our base camp at Kadugli was used as the central transit point for personnel rotating out or returning from leave or visits to other outlying camps. Accommodation was at a premium and it was understood that if you were away on leave your bed might be used by someone passing through. We had very few women on the team and since I had my own hut it was generally the case that any of the ladies would be put there if I was away. During one such absence, when I was on leave or visiting Kenya or somewhere, Cordelia, a lady police officer seconded from a northern European country, passed through the camp en route home on leave. Overnight she was given my bed but no one thought to mention Lizzie. To be fair, very few other people even knew about Lizzie so I must take some responsibility for what happened but Cordelia should certainly have taken more care putting up her mosquito net. During the night Lizzie had begun her mosquito-hunting night patrol but as she stepped out on to the top of the net it started sinking down to come to rest on the bosom of the lady below. Poor Cordelia awoke to find herself wrapped in the collapsed net with a monster lizard nestling into her décolletage and tasting the air around her face. I was told later that Cordelia's scream woke most of the camp including Verges, my neighbour in the next hut who rushed to her rescue, freed her from entanglement and beat poor Lizzie to death.

My deputy met me at the airstrip a few days later and reluctantly told me what had happened. Cordelia had gone but left a note to say *Sorry*. I had my first bout of malaria a month later. (I've since found out that the colouring indicates that 'Lizzie' was a male but, after more than ten years, it's too late to rename him.)

*

If you accept that living long-term in Africa will mean, inevitably, getting malaria sooner or later you must also accept that treatment is inevitable. Years before, while taking regular weekly doses of mefloquine before travelling to Ghana I had experienced some very odd dreams the following night. These were not the kind of nightmares many of my colleagues had but rather more like being in a very real Alice in Wonderland world. I had been told that the drug simply intensifies whatever type of personality is inside the patient's head to start with, so I'll leave you to work out what that says about me; this was all on one pill per week, remember.

I started noticing symptoms rather like ordinary flu. I had a raised temperature and was sweating a bit more than usual but I was in a hot country and it was the wet season. My joints ached and I felt tired. The medical officer said I probably just needed a couple of paracetamol but wanted to get a blood test done first. Today there are tests that can be done easily in the field but at that time I needed to get to a clinic. It couldn't be done in the camp so I had one of the mechanics and Mohammed drive me into Kadugli in a pickup truck. The clinic turned out to be a private facility which doubled as a garage workshop but this was the height of the malaria season so the technician wasn't taking bookings for car repairs. Having got his blood sample he sat me down to wait for the results. I don't actually recall going outside but the next thing I do remember was waking up curled in a foetal position in the back of the pickup with my head resting on the spare wheel. All around the sides of the truck were laughing and giggling children trying to get the *Hawajah* to wake up. Mohammed was beaming down among them to tell me, "It is wonderful news, Mr Dogberry. You have millions of parasites. You have very good malaria." I wouldn't have wanted to receive bad news from Mohammed if this counted as 'wonderful'.

Malaria is rather like a 'Boil-in-the-Bag' meal where you are the food and the bag is your own skin. You will become more tired than you can imagine but unable to sleep and about the second day, death starts to feel like a really attractive option. Every part of your body, every joint, patch of skin or movement is intensely painful as water erupts through the skin like squeezing out a sponge. Then comes the medic with the mefloquine. Not a single pill once per week, but half a dozen in one dose with pints and pints of water. Then comes sleep. The next day, more of the same until, after a few days, your temperature reduces to mere scorching and you become vaguely aware that you are not dead. Now, imagine what sort of dreams you will have after perhaps ten times the weekly dose in just forty-eight hours. I was living in a hut, in fact a repurposed cargo container, furnished with a bed, chair and desk plus my equipment locker. When I came back to earth I was still in my bed and all the furniture was in place. My bush hat was even over the back of the chair; I remembered that kind of detail. But the walls had disappeared and I could see across to the motor workshop, from the parade ground to the mess hall and birds in the trees over my head. I saw that people I knew were walking past but it didn't occur to me to question why they took no notice of my bed out in the open. Also walking past was Lizzie, fully restored to health but now about twenty-five feet long and six feet high on his day off from filming *Jurassic Park*. At the time, all this seemed perfectly normal. Why shouldn't a giant lizard be walking around the camp? What's so odd about the walls of my hut vanishing? Gradually over the next few days I became more aware of what was happening around me. My colleagues made sure I drank as much water as I needed, which was a great deal more than I wanted, and kept me supplied with fresh fruit and plain bread until I was strong enough to eat in the mess hall again. If you go to work in Africa, either take the tablets or keep nervous Nordic lady police officers away from your pet lizard.

XI

Talking Peace

Sudan Peace Negotiations (Naivasha)

By the time I arrived in the JMM in July 2002 the peace talks were well under way and it was clear that an agreement would be reached after the final wrinkles had been ironed out. Some months after my arrival a question arose concerning the role of police in a peaceful and democratic society and after much umming and ahing a request was made, through the appropriate diplomatic channels, for Police Advisor Dogberry to pop down to Kenya and give the delegates the benefit of his wisdom, knowledge and experience. Some days later my head of mission, a very experienced senior military officer, asked me what I thought of their question and told me to get packed for a few weeks away. I said I could probably knock off a reply in a day or so and he should expect me back by the weekend. I was wrong; he was right.

From the forward base camp in Kadugli, I had to travel to our HQ in Khartoum. That meant a bumpy ride in an elderly Antonov (incidentally the only aircraft I've ever seen that could do a three-point turn under its own power at the end of a grass airstrip) to the international airport in the city. After an overnight stay I bought a ticket to Nairobi and travelled the next day, busily working on my erudite and profound answer to the problem that had been causing the negotiators to lose so much sleep. The next day I flew to Kenya to be met by a driver who took me to a hotel in the city promising to return the next day to drive me to the Naivasha Valley. He turned up the next morning not in the little Fiat he'd been driving at the airport but in a nice new Land Rover 110 which allowed lots of room for my one small rucksack, briefcase and bottle of duty-free whisky.

Naivasha is in the Rift Valley about sixty miles north of Nairobi. A very large chunk of Africa, about a quarter of the continent, is trying to break away and drift off into the Indian Ocean but that's not going to happen any time soon and, in the meantime, house prices have not been depressed while some stunning scenery has been created. Leaving Nairobi behind we passed through progressively more rural villages, some surrounded by forest and banana plantations, others by the largest fields of flowers I could imagine which were harvested daily, processed, wrapped, boxed, driven to Nairobi, flown to Heathrow and put in buckets for sale at petrol stations along the M4 within hours. Some places had names like 'Brackenhurst' that might have been in Devon; others definitely not, such as 'Kijabe'.

I had my introduction to what it means to stay in tourist rural Africa when we arrived in the hotel car park. A police car was parked across the gate with two policemen pretending to pay attention – high-level diplomatic talks were being held here after all but the armed guards I saw wandering around were, in fact, employed by the hotel for the safety of the guests. A bit of knife-point robbery was not unknown and the risk from baboons and other local wildlife was not insignificant. The car park itself was supervised by a very helpful old man assisted by a six-foot-tall young ostrich. I hadn't seen this bird at first and became aware of it only when I felt a gentle tap on my shoulder as I reached in the back for my briefcase. This inquisitive but very polite and friendly animal had come over to us immediately the doors opened and put his head inside, a long way inside, to inspect the car, me, all my pockets and luggage before reporting back to the car park attendant that we were okay to stay. He then went back to stand beside the attendant's sentry box and await the next arrival.

The peace negotiations had completely taken over a tourist lodge hotel complex beside Lake Naivasha where the chairman, delegates and support staff had been eagerly awaiting my arrival. Or so I thought. The chairman was expecting me but not for another day or two and suggested I just settle in before meeting the delegates who were taking a couple of days off to rest.

The reception assistant took me to my lodge which was modelled on a local style circular mud-brick and thatch hut called a 'rondavel'. Apparently, this was originally a South African word from Afrikaans and I came across it throughout much of sub-Saharan Africa but no village hut ever had a bedroom, luxury bathroom and sitting room large enough to play tennis. When he opened the door, I thought that either the housekeeper hadn't made up the room from the previous guest or else it had been burgled. The bed had been stripped and the covers spread over the chairs and TV. The bathroom was a disaster zone. The hotel's very generous range of soaps, creams and shampoos had been squirted around and smeared over the toilet, bath and mirrors with the shower left running. The receptionist just shrugged and telephoned housekeeping to sort it out and left me to get unpacked, a process that took about thirty seconds. Two housekeepers arrived a couple of minutes later and the older, a lady of about 175, berated her junior colleague in a language I could not even begin to make out – I'd never heard Swahili spoken before. Between scoldings she told me, in highly accented English, that the room had been made up earlier but a tiny window had been left open and that had been too tempting an invitation for the monkeys which had then greatly enjoyed themselves before my arrival. Would I please be kind enough to make sure I closed and locked all the windows whenever I went out? I promised I would. I'd spent the previous three months sleeping under a mosquito net in a forward base camp where I shared my hut with a large lizard and I was very happy indeed to adapt to five-star diplomacy for as long as it took.

*

It appeared I was expected to make a presentation and had nothing to do now except draft it and prepare some handout notes. A lot of resources had been put into bringing me there and I believed in giving value for money. Outside my lodge was my private terrace looking down across rolling green lawns and Acacia trees. At least I think they were Acacia trees. If it turns out Acacia trees don't grow in this part of Africa please refer to Mrs Dogberry who will confirm that I can't tell the difference between a rose and an onion. Different brands of tree are completely outside my area of expertise.

I settled into a chair in the sunshine with a bottle of Tusker Beer from the well-stocked fridge. The two African beers I came across most frequently were Tusker and Star Lager. Both were very good and reliably sterile but Star didn't actually have anything on the label to show how strong it was. I suspect this was because the company couldn't be sure from one production run to the next so it could be anything from almost a non-alcoholic beer substitute to extremely strong. It introduced a sort of Russian Roulette atmosphere in the bar in the evening not knowing if a different box had been opened. I started making some preliminary notes and nibbling on a piece of fruit from the bucket-sized complimentary fruit bowl. A tribe of about fifteen hotel burglary suspect monkeys was scampering around in the grounds outside my terrace. What type of monkeys? I'm ashamed to admit I don't know but they had tails so I think I'm safe in saying they were monkeys not apes and I've watched enough BBC Four and Sir David Attenborough to guess they were probably a family group. The small ones were just beginning to play together away from their mothers and when I lobbed an apple towards them it was always caught deftly and gone in a second. That was a mistake. The whole group started to work their way towards me fielding the various bits of fruit I shied at them and they seemed very cute until I ran out of ammunition. One of the females looked at me from about twenty yards away, drew herself up to about three feet tall and screamed, baring a set of teeth of which any tiger would have been proud. In the distance I could see a much larger chap taking an interest who should have been wearing a T-shirt with ALPHA MALE across the chest. Time to go inside and make sure the windows were secure.

I met my friends (monkeys and colleagues) again the next morning when I went for breakfast in the main-building restaurant. The monkeys seemed to have forgotten me but were keeping the other guests amused and the staff busy. Two small youngsters had come in through the wide open sliding doors which led out to the pool and were running around in the restaurant to keep the waiters distracted while the rest of the tribe came in and almost stripped the breakfast buffet, then sat on the roof throwing bits of melon skin into the pool. They'd been there for thousands of years before the hotel had been built so they probably felt they had some proprietary rights.

The other animals with proprietary rights were the hippos which came up out of Lake Naivasha and settled on the hotel golf course in the evening. I don't play golf but I assume the rules include something about one-ton dangerous animals impeding play. I walked down to the lake one evening following the path just to kill some time before meeting the other observers to the peace talks in the bar. The hippos ignored me and I ignored them and made my way back to the hotel after about an hour. I mentioned this later to one of the delegates and he told me that only mosquitoes and soldiers kill more people in Africa than hippos. They can run amazingly fast for such a large animal and, apparently, getting between a baby hippo and its mother is exceedingly dangerous. They can't climb trees but neither can I although I suspect being chased by a hippo might provide just the motivation to learn. I didn't go again.

After a couple of days of this less than frantic activity I was invited to a session of the negotiations when 'Security' was on the agenda which was code for 'Mr Dogberry's presentation'. I had been allocated an hour and, after some polite questions, finished and was thanked for my time. My speaking notes were distributed and I went to get packed, fully expecting to be gone in the morning. In fact, I did make the later flight from Nairobi the next day but had been warned that I would probably be asked back. "Yes, of course, Excellency." In fact, I got to know Jomo Kenyatta Airport quite well over the next two or three years.

Hell's Gate Park and Mt Longonot

Naturalist Joy Adamson wrote about hand-rearing Elsa the lioness in her book *Born Free*[4] which was made into a film in 1966. The main gate of Hell's Gate National Park, which was used as the setting for the film, was a short walk from the hotel but although there were lots of zebra and giraffe, there were no lions by then. That's probably quite fortunate as the best way to get around was on a bike rented from the hotel. It's a place where the Rift Valley looks as if it was formed last month. A vast area of land has simply dropped down leaving sheer cliffs on three sides and zebra wandered with complete contempt for tourists on bicycles and only came near when they were trying to steal something – anything – whether they really wanted it or not. If you find yourself in this area and see a baby zebra keep well away. Mum will be somewhere close by; she will not appreciate your attention and will kick you out of the park before you can explain. Actually, the same applies to most animals in Africa, especially hippos which are just mean to everyone.

Herds of giraffe practised their dignified walk and sneered at us from on high. The young males lived in the herd until the top alpha male decided they were not wanted, then they were pushed out until they'd developed enough attitude to make a bid for top job. That left them with a bit of a problem in the meantime. They're naturally herd animals and feel safer in groups but no other herd would be prepared to accept a stranger. I have no idea if the local solution has been replicated elsewhere but in Hell's Gate lonely adolescent giraffe lived

4   *Born Free*. Joy Adamson; published by Pantheon Books (1960).

comfortably among herds of zebra. The arrangement worked well for both; the zebra A+ didn't regard the newcomer as a challenger and the giraffes had company and safety in return for acting as a high-level lookout for danger. "Why are you pointing that camera at me? Haven't you ever seen a zebra before? I'm a zebra, I'm a zebra!"

*

Eventually I teamed up with some of the UN and diplomatic observers assigned to the negotiations as we all had a lot of spare time on our hands. I've always had 'Climb a Volcano' on my bucket list and the Kenyan Ministry of Tourism had obligingly put Mount Longonot within easy reach of the hotel. As volcanoes go this one was designed with tourists like me in mind. It's a gentle slope almost to the top, then suddenly gets quite steep but is still a reasonably easy climb. From a distance the rock is just grey and rugged but in most places it's compressed ash and feels like extremely abrasive, very fine sand. I never wore shorts in Africa – or anywhere else – but some of my colleagues went for style over practicality and had blisters that took weeks to heal after the ash got down into their boots. From the rim there were a couple of places where puffs of steam were venting and the ancient flows down into the valley were very distinct. At the hotel I was told that the volcano was dormant and had not erupted for tens of thousands of years but I've since found out that a more accurate date is probably 1860; another of those things it's better not to know at the time.

Inside the cone, the floor is lush green and home to a population of baboons which were best left alone. Baboons, like trees, come in a variety of models usually very specific to the area where they live and well adapted to local conditions. They share one thing in common, however, no matter how much we might think we like them and are prepared to share our planet with them, they don't like us. They have very good reason for their hostility as until relatively recently, and even now illegally, they have been hunted mercilessly for 'sport', sometimes for meat but most often to clear them away from areas where farming or other human activity is in conflict. Depending on the local type, baboons might be anything from a little larger than the local apes to almost human size. Males are much larger and fiercer. Challenged in their own territory, tribe leaders will stand their ground and attack with total determination. They do not mean to scare you away (unless you happen to be another baboon), they mean to kill and, probably, eat you. Unfortunately, they've not read the section in the Baboon Tribe Leaders' Handbook about spears, arrows and firearms. Spears and arrows were generally not too much of a problem as people learned how to live in ways and places that didn't bring them into conflict but firearms were a different matter. Contrary to popular belief, bullets don't lift the victim off their feet in dramatic cinematic style and even humans who don't know they have been injured will sometimes carry on doing what they had been doing until they've been hit several more times. Baboons haven't seen enough Clint Eastwood films to know that they are supposed to fall over when they're shot so a lot of ammunition is needed. Sadly, in most places in Africa, a lot of ammunition is available. It was their volcano and I was quite happy to leave them to enjoy it.

*

International negotiations were conducted like the mating rituals of elephants. The really important matters happened at very high level accompanied by much trumpeting and roaring and took months to produce results but as advances were made the negotiations eventually moved to Nairobi. We no longer needed the facilities of an entire tourist resort hotel and in the end all that was left was to finalise the wording of the agreement and sort out the highly sensitive seating plan for the signing ceremony. We were nearly there but still needed a couple more weeks.

Between drafting sessions there was still some free time and when the British High Commission was kind enough to allow the use of a minibus and driver half a dozen of us took the opportunity to get away from the city. Nairobi National Park is to the south of the city and from the city side looks like an enclosed area with an entrance gate, restaurant and, of course, a gift shop, but is open to the African bush on the other side. From the gate it was rather like driving in Windsor Great Park. Roads inside the park were well maintained and signposted and for the first half an hour we only saw a couple of antelope from a very long way off. The signpost to the 'Picnic Area' took us towards solid benches and tables but before we got there a very large black warthog dashed across the road about twenty-five yards in front of us followed by two lions. It had no chance and was taken down in the grass. It took us by surprise, although probably not as much as it did the warthog. This was classic nature at the 'red in tooth and claw' end and it was fascinating to watch as four, possibly more, lions dismantled and ate every part of their kill over the next hour. They didn't seem at all perturbed by our presence and a couple of them glanced over as if to invite us to join them. After their lunch they wandered off and disappeared into the long grass leaving just a red stain on the ground which was itself soon being picked over by birds. The rest of the day was quite an anticlimax. A large buffalo ignored us. Half a dozen zebra appeared on the horizon but didn't want to come near; most of us had already seen zebra in Hell's Gate Park anyway. The official picnic area no longer seemed like a good idea as it was somewhat uncertain who it was meant for – can lions read signs in English? When I'm reincarnated, I don't want to be a warthog in Kenya.

Back in the drafting session a couple of days later I mentioned our day off to a British expat who had lived in Nairobi with her family for fifteen years. She had been to the national park at least once a month with her husband and two young children and often used the picnic area. In all that time she had never even seen a lion, much less an actual kill by a gang of them.

*

Just about all visitors to Nairobi make at least one visit to 'Carnivore'. If you have been there you can skip the next two paragraphs. If you're a vegetarian you should certainly jump to the end of this chapter now. Carnivore is a restaurant specialising in various kinds of 'bush' meat – there's a clue in the name. We arrived in a group of about ten and were shown to a very large circular table. The head waiter put up a small flag showing that the table was in use then left us to get a wooden plate, knives, forks and salad from the buffet. There was no menu. Waiters patrolled the tables carrying huge chunks of roast meat on three-foot-long steel spikes and a long jungle knife which looked sharp enough to shave with. When a waiter came to the table, he would announce "Giraffe – Hoowantsum" and stick the spike in the table while he carved off thick slabs of meat. A colleague would then come past and repeat the procedure with haunches of warthog (very good, by the way), ostrich (like beef), crocodile (a bit like chicken) or anything else that had been silly enough to wander into the hunter's cross-hairs. All the time the flag stayed upright the waiters kept coming.

All this took place outdoors and although I don't recall if there was a cabaret I remember Doctor Dawa quite clearly. Tusker Beer was available but most relied on Doctor Dawa's medicine. He was a very tall chap dressed in a formal black tail coat, Manchester United supporters' T-shirt, white tennis shorts, white top hat with a long feather in the hatband and flip-flops. He carried a tray on a strap round his shoulder filled with ice, a couple of bottles of rum (I think – although it might possibly have been petrol) and a huge pot of rich dark honey. No matter what you asked for, what you got was a Doctor Dawa Cocktail. This involved filling a glass with ice, putting in a 6' piece of bamboo dipped generously in the honey then topped off with whatever it was in the bottle. I've still got the bamboo sticks and I've tried to replicate the mixture several times with varying degrees of success. Tesco just doesn't sell African honey the colour of chocolate.

XII

UN Speak

2005

On 9th January 2005, the Sudan People's Liberation Movement and the government of Sudan signed the Comprehensive Peace Agreement and a line was drawn under one of the most complex and protracted conflicts in Africa. We breathed a sigh of relief and looked forward to a positive future until on 30th July 2005 'Doctor John' Garang was killed when his helicopter crashed and it all started over again.

It had always been understood that as soon as the Comprehensive Peace Agreement was signed, the next stage would be a UN Security Council Resolution and deployment of a new UN mission. UNSCR 1590 was adopted unanimously on 24th March 2005 and the United Nations Mission in Sudan (UNMIS) was established. Once that had been done the secretary general, Kofi Anan in those days, appointed his special representative (the SRSG) to lead the mission. This is a very senior diplomatic appointment equivalent to ambassador and often with powers in the country over the 'host' government. The secretary general also appoints the head of the military component and the head of the police component, always called the UN police commissioner. Any former police officer, no matter how 'retired' he or she may believe themselves to be, will be tempted back into uniform at the offer of being appointed commissioner of police in one of the largest countries in Africa. When the offer came, in September 2004, I gave it careful consideration for about three milliseconds and said, "Yes, please."

United Nations Headquarters, New York

Welcome and 'In-Briefing' to New UN Personnel

"Good morning, ladies, gentlemen and those who choose not to identify by gender specifics. My name is Stockleigh Pomeroy and this session is to welcome you to UNP. All of you here will work in DPKO. If you are under the impression that you are headed for WHO, HCR or HCHR go down the hall and get a ticket for GVA. If you are 'ESCO you should have been at CDG yesterday. Have a nice day and goodbye. This a.m. we'll cover IT, IF and TA; p.m. you'll hear from ICRC about IT, POW and from HCR about IDPs. Also, MSF, IGOs and NGOs. Wherever you end up you can expect your AoR to be affected by APM, UXO, DPU, CW and IT. If we have time we might cover IT in the RF and CIS…"

This was my first real day with the United Nations. I had been recruited in Africa but the selection had been endorsed by HMG – sorry, old habit, I mean Her Majesty's Government. I found out later, over a beer in a bar near Central Park, that it was usual for Stockleigh to drone on like this in his mid-Atlantic monotone for hours at a time. At least one other newbie fell asleep and paid the price of waking up, cold and abandoned, in a pitch-black lecture hall. By eleven o'clock I was ready to gnaw off my foot out of boredom when Stockleigh called a coffee break and we all trooped down to the terrace on UN Plaza. This is without doubt the best place for coffee and doughnuts in New York. Service, quality and prices are high, high and low respectively and safety is assured by at least half a dozen armed security officers. Being a DPKO group we tended to be from a wide variety of countries of origin but shared two things in common. We were about thirty-five years older than most other UN recruits and we'd all been around the block a few times.

Some of us were destined to be police commissioners in different United Nations Missions and the others would be working in New York. We also shared in common that we had understood almost nothing of what Stockleigh had said, mainly because our only common language was English while Stockleigh was speaking 'Unnese'. Unnese sounds like English but is so heavily loaded with acronyms as to be a barrier to, rather than a channel of, communication. It's very similar to Redcrossian which is like Franglaise but again with that larding of acronyms.

We'd all been too polite on our first day in the organisation to make waves but had to do something to brighten the rest of the day. During the next session and until lunch, Stockleigh didn't get away with introducing any acronym without one of us asking what it meant. He had to slow his pace of delivery as a result and never got down to talking about IT in the RF and CIS. Lunch was probably as much a relief to him as it was to us. The sad thing was that even Stockleigh himself was unable to decipher most of the terms he'd used when challenged.

Over the next couple of years I became quite fluent in Unnese myself but resisted using it as much as possible. Acronyms breed like fleas. You might want to glance through the glossary of acronyms at the end and see how many you can slip into conversation. Two points for getting one in unchallenged. Over twenty-five points qualifies you for a job in New York but the list is endless.

*

The United Nations Mission in Sudan, like all UN missions, offices and outposts, was always referred to by its acronym used as a spoken word. Thus, it was "*Unmis*" and not U-N-M-I-S. It was an entity with full diplomatic status so we were located in the capital but were still in the early set-up phase when I joined. For the first few weeks we worked from a hotel in Khartoum but very quickly established bases in Juba in the south and elsewhere. Within weeks of arrival the mission had its own fleet of aircraft to take goods and personnel wherever they had to go as well as running convoys over such roads as existed and even some very slow barges doing the six-week trip along the White Nile from Khartoum to Juba. The White Nile, from the south, and the Blue Nile, from Ethiopia in the east, meet at Khartoum to become the Nile. Shortly before finding my first apartment in Khartoum I had a room and office in the HQ hotel overlooking the confluence of these two rivers. They are not blue and white but the waters are distinctly different and don't really mix properly for the next couple of miles. At some stages of the year the flow from the south in the White Nile can be so much stronger that the Blue Nile actually reverses and runs back towards Ethiopia for a short while.[5]

Khartoum was a city I already knew quite well after more than two years in Sudan but, unlike the JMM, I had to find my own accommodation. And if you think prices can rise quickly at home try renting an apartment in any city where a new international mission has arrived. Good liveable quarters could be found but rents rocketed with the arrival of the Blue Helmets. I eventually found a reasonably good, modern flat with air conditioning – as vital to life as water – for under $350 (USD) per month. I stayed about three weeks before I moved because the loudspeakers on the mosque opposite were just ten feet from my bedroom window. I had to move my flat a couple of times in fact and each time the price went up. My final landlord was quite laid back about having a *Hawajah* tenant so long as I paid in advance and didn't leave whisky bottles where his wives could see them. He was a most accommodating chap and was always quite happy to help me make sure they were empty. Tenants

---

5   To know more of the region I strongly recommend *The Life of My Choice* by Wilfred Thesiger.

in this kind of accommodation, which had modern furniture and air conditioning, tended to be internationals, either UN or from any of the other aid agencies which sprout like mushrooms. Most of the diplomatic missions, certainly from the wealthier countries, tended to supply their senior staff with accommodation to ensure that it was of a suitable standard and safe. Some, on the other hand, let their third secretaries and consular officers live in the sort of place I did.

*

The flat immediately below mine was the 'residence' of the deputy head of mission at his country's embassy, I'll call him Mossi, where he lived with his family. He was a very friendly sort who did his best to make sure that his six children didn't disturb the neighbourhood too much. I had arranged to have exclusive use of the yard of the house so I could get my big white UN 4x4 off the street at night. Coming out one Friday morning on what was a working day for me but a day off for just about everyone else, I met Mossi in the yard demonstrating to number 3 son the correct way to despatch a goat ready for the family feast in the evening. Mossi had their doomed main course gripped firmly between his knees and held the horns with one hand and a knife like a twelve-inch curved razor in the other. Number 3, about twelve years old, was watching intently and didn't notice me at first but his father did. Just at the wrong moment he looked up, gave me a big grin and said, "Wonderful to see you Mr Dogberry. I hope you are well." However, his arm was already moving and what should have been a clean kill became a very messy one as my car was liberally drenched and by the time I got to my office in the UN compound, about half a mile away, was covered with a thick layer of black flies. I handed my keys to my driver, Omar, to get the car washed and just hoped the yard had been hosed down by the time I went home.

Omar was one of the first native Khartoum residents I met when I moved to the capital. He was given his job as my driver on the basis of his solid qualifications, namely that his brother-in-law worked in the security department. The fact that he didn't actually hold a driving licence was sort of missed until I asked to see it and was eventually shown one issued the previous day – even my Sudanese driving licence was older than that. But Omar was good company and useful in many ways. His English was very good having worked in an American company and it was helpful to have him listening quietly at the back of meetings to let me know later whether my interpreter was editing what I was being told too much and what the other drivers talked about around their oil-drum campfire in the yard including gossip about other expats. Was he also reporting sideways to the GoS and GoSS security services? Almost certainly. I gave Omar a pair of Ray Ban Wayfarer sunglasses which made him look like Sam Cooke. Unfortunately, he also drove like Sam Cooke but I was quite happy to drive myself most of the time.

*

My remit was to establish the police component of the mission under the terms of the Security Council Resolution which had conjured us into existence. I would eventually have command of more than a thousand police officers drawn from over thirty contributing nations and speaking more languages than that between them as well as the common language of the mission – English. Rates of pay for police around the world vary enormously as do conditions for secondment to UN missions. The UN pays a very generous 'per diem' allowance (in USD in cash) to cover living expenses and it was often much more than many of my officers received in salary at home. A three-year UN job would sometimes set them up for life and they usually cut their 'in-country' living expenses to the bone to save money. I knew of as many as twelve sharing an apartment and living very frugally indeed. They were usually also prepared to put national and political differences at home aside while the dollars rolled in. I had officers from countries in conflict working alongside others who had been shooting each other across a border just weeks before. Some countries actually stopped payment of salary at home while their personnel were in the mission but it was still financially worth their while to be there.

Unhelpfully there is no UN police uniform and all officers wore the uniform of their own country but with the addition of a blue UN beret or helmet and a UN decal on the sleeve. Individual roles within the mission were allocated by my head of personnel on my behalf but officers still wore their rank insignia from home. This could cause confusion, and sometimes a little resentment. When a deputy director general, wearing insignia which would have marked him as equivalent to a major general in the army, found himself assigned to a location where there had already been assigned a very experienced and competent woman sergeant from the Caribbean as team leader, he was a little miffed – but not so miffed that he was prepared to forego the UN per diem and he drove the patrol cars anyway.

Without doubt the most impressive were the contingent which arrived from Fiji. These were all giants whose uniform included their traditional 'sulu', a sort of long kilt usually with deep points along the bottom edge. I was told it was introduced for men and women as a result of European colonisation in the nineteenth century having been imported from Tonga by missionaries and originally worn to indicate their conversion to Christianity (and spare the missionaries' wives blushes as a result of any immodest display). It is now regarded as Fiji's national dress and included in the uniforms of both military and police.

As a former detective I first had to get used to wearing a uniform again and for a long while that felt like being a mixture of hotel doorman and chorus-line player from *HMS Pinafore* – we are talking about a great deal of silver braid. The thing I found most difficult to adapt to, but tried hard and eventually accepted without laughing too much, was being addressed as 'Excellency'. It grows on you after a while – a bit like when my son and daughter-in-law were expecting their first baby and asked if I wanted to be called 'Granddad'. I told them I was comfortable with 'Sir'. Best get things off to a proper start, eh?

*

Country X, which seconded their officers to our mission, also made its police force responsible for the issue of driving licences at home; actually, this is a very common arrangement internationally. (A stringent test or a $10 gift is usually the going rate.) It was a condition of service that all officers must be competent in English, have a current pistol qualification and hold a driving licence for manual transmission cars. My chief of staff, an officer from a northern European country with many years of international experience, came into my office one morning smiling broadly, always a warning sign. He said that ten officers from X had arrived overnight and dropped ten shiny new driving licences on my desk. All had been issued four days before and had consecutive serial numbers. Driving check-tests were arranged to take place over the coming few days during their induction training. A morning came when District Commissioner Y, a rank roughly equivalent to brigadier at home, came into my office and, snapping to attention, made a salute so stiff that his arm quivered like a watch spring. He told me that he had the honour to inform me that he had failed his driving test. It seems he had probably never in his life been in a vehicle without a chauffeur and while he had managed to get the Nissan Patrol moving, he had not apparently read the bit in the owner's manual about steering or braking. Steering had become irrelevant, however, when he had hit a local bus.

To avoid diplomatic problems, it was arranged that he receive a week of driver training and have a second test. That took place on Friday a week later at a time when the faithful would be at prayer and the streets empty. This time he managed nearly a whole kilometre before he was drawn to another bus like a moth to a flame. I couldn't afford the cars – or buses – and it was cheaper just to give him a job as head of pencil sharpening at headquarters. Problem solved.

To Help You Come Back

I have quite a collection of walking sticks at home, some of which, sadly, I now have to use. There is a tradition in Sudan, perhaps elsewhere in Africa as well, that a guest who is welcome is given a walking stick, "...to help you come back." I always thought this was a touching gesture and the sticks I have range from the simplest wooden ones to an elaborately carved and decorated one in extremely hard black ebony. Military and police officers have a similar tradition but hand over batons instead, again sometimes highly decorated; I have several of those too. After settling in to Khartoum I went down to Omdurman one day – the two cities have effectively merged into one – and found a wood-turner. I told him what I needed and he'd knocked out twenty-five ebony batons by the time I went back next day. Along the street, which probably hadn't changed since General Gordon's day, I found a silversmith who copied my UN cap badge to go on the end of the batons. I went back a few days later to collect them and when I asked about the cost, he simply weighed them. After that, whenever I went to a meeting I put one under my arm ready to exchange if I was offered the one carried by my host. Of the original twenty-five, I have one left here in the UK, I gave a couple to expat friends but all the rest ended up tucked under the arms of GoS or GoSS senior officers. The UN didn't hold with such fripperies, and certainly wouldn't have been prepared to pay for them so I paid myself. Individually handmade and silver mounted, the total cost came to about $150 which I thought was very good value for money.

Wind and Weather

Some of you may have heard that the weather in Sudan is not quite what you'd expect in Devon – well, not yet anyway but give global warming a chance, eh? Having been to Africa before, when I arrived in Khartoum from London, I knew I was in Africa as soon as the aircraft door was cracked open. The air had a distinct aroma, almost a taste, to it; not unpleasant but uniquely African. There're two seasons instead of the four we're used to. Don't think in terms of summer and winter. There's just hot and wet – roughly November/December to April/May – followed by hot and dry.

When the rains started in earnest, humidity in the air went from zero to over a hundred per cent. It was probably a little cooler, down to about thirty degrees at night but it still felt like sleeping in a sauna. Rain fell so hard it lashed across the shoulders like a whip but it rarely lasted more than half an hour at a time and some days it might not rain at all although days like that were few. Travel relied on flying again as the roads quickly became impassable. Mosquitos swarmed at night and precautions against malaria had to be rigidly observed. Nets had to be inspected thoroughly for holes every day and sleeping quarters were constantly fumigated by smoking with slow-burning chemical cords. Periodically, we were treated to a visit by the 'killer'. This was obviously one of our own personnel but I never found out who it was. Dressed in a full-body white HAZMAT suit, plus a full-face mask and hood, he went through every building, inside and out, with a two-stroke petrol-driven blower on his back pumping out a thick white smoke that smelled and tasted like a mixture of diesel and liquorice.

The dry season brought temperatures up in the fifties and a desiccating wind. There might be the odd shower but these were rare and called 'lucky rain'. The ground baked to something like concrete but, if you knew where to dig, it was possible to find muddy brown water deep below which was enough to keep the cattle, goats and camels alive. Roads became useable again with care as the deep ruts and furrows were flattened into a hard sandy surface. Because the air was so dry, taking shelter out of the sun made it immediately feel cooler; this close to the equator the sun was almost vertical and a wide-brimmed hat supplied almost all the shade you'd need although when I moved over to the UN and back into uniform I didn't even have this luxury as the uniform headgear was either a beret or helmet.

The wide plains of grass, which had been over three feet high last week, became yellow and bare. Fires wiped away huge areas of grazing land. Sometimes these were natural but others were started deliberately by settled villagers to dissuade nomadic tribes of cattle/camel/goat herders from passing through and taking all the available water and forage, even crops, to feed their animals.

Our huts were raised on concrete blocks to keep them about a foot off the ground and as a result water collected underneath during the rainy season. These cool(er) wet pools provided perfect breeding grounds for mosquitos and many other sorts of insects, lizards and frogs. The frogs especially seemed to be on minimum hours contracts and appeared together in a wave over a couple of days. They would usually stay under the huts in the shade during the day but if something made them come out, such as one of the resident feral camp cats, they rarely got far. In the heat, two or three hops was about average before they simply died where they landed. Some were picked up almost straight away by small eagles but even the ones which dried out were taken later. It was fascinating to watch a bird of prey pick up a dried frog from the ground and fly to the water pump and drop it in the mud by the trough then stand guard over it for five minutes while it re-hydrated before taking it off for a picnic.

*

As the rains got closer there were dry thunderstorms which could light up the sky all night but without releasing a single drop of water. This was also when to be ready for sandstorms which were the most dramatic weather events I've ever seen. Against an otherwise clear blue sky what looked like a range of hills that shouldn't have been there would appear on the horizon forming a reddish-brown cliff face stretching for perhaps thirty miles and rising to 2,000 feet or more advancing at anything from ten to thirty miles per hour. Our pilots were naturally wary about being caught in the open and having to fly into a sandstorm and would generally try to fly over it or around it, or even turn back. As a last resort a helicopter might have to land and cover all the engine ports and other open vents and just wait for it to pass. I was never in the air during a sandstorm but several times I had to stop on the road. It's not that it wasn't possible to see – visibility was sometimes quite good – but the fine desert sand could destroy an engine in about ten minutes unless you stopped and switched off quickly and covered all the air intakes. As the storm passed over you would suddenly find yourself in a world of intense red light. The sun was still there but now it was just a bright red disc against a dull red sky. And there you had to stay until it passed over and was gone. That might be anything from twenty minutes to more than a couple of hours. Longer sandstorms were known but were unusual although most people had stories about storms that lasted for days. When it passed it would sometimes be followed by a rain front which could flood the roads in seconds, instantly filling the *wadis* and ponds to overflowing.

From my office in Khartoum I watched in awe as a sandstorm passed over the city. This one was too early in the year to be followed by rain and after half an hour the sun was shining again. I got back to my flat that evening to find that I had left a small window open in the kitchen. Every level surface in my apartment was now covered with about an inch of fine brown powdery grit – the floors, furniture, my bed, kitchen and bathroom, wardrobes and cupboards, clothes, computer and TV. My landlord came up with his wife and sons to help me clear up and we took out enough sand for a respectable beach. All the bedding and clothes had to be washed but things were never really the same again. My TV and laptop were useless. Always close the windows; it's not just monkeys that cause problems.

*

Sudan was a country in which the culture and, especially, all aspects of law were dominated by Islamic culture and law including a total ban on the production, importation, sale, possession or consumption of alcoholic drink. Well, so the authorities would have you think. Among some, strict observance was obviously more a matter of faith than compliance with mere secular regulations. When our medical unit at Kadugli gave first aid to one of the local staff who had malaria and fainted splitting his lip very badly, a medic had swabbed his skin to give him an injection. Within minutes we nearly had a riot among our local employees as word went round that an alcohol cleansing swab had been used and we had to have a senior village elder read the small print on the packet. Feelings ran very high. In other places, especially the more rural villages, everything from sorghum beer to home-distilled spirit was freely available. I visited the local police commander one morning in Kadugli and saw a policeman, outside in the sun, doing extra drill in full kit who was being punished for being drunk on duty.

Khartoum wasn't quite like Chicago and New York during prohibition with speakeasy bars but those who knew where to go could always get a drink. The city had long had a large expat community involved in all sorts of industry, consultancy, training and commerce but the most rapidly expanding group was in the oil industry. Most worked out in the field, of course, but even these frequently visited the capital creating a huge market for illicit booze and huge markets will always attract business. Imagine going out any day to eat at a Chinese restaurant in Sudan with your working colleagues and friends. Maybe ten of you relax around the typical circular table while familiar Cantonese and Sichuan food is laid out; at every elbow is a large pot of tea. I hadn't been aware that oil drillers were such devoted tea drinkers but these men could not only get through three or four pots each over a meal, they guarded their personal pot with a heavily muscled and tattooed arm. Always men, of course. While women were allowed in public restaurants only a very few expats actually ever did so and Sudanese women, never. What about enforcement? The police tried hard to address this flagrant disregard of the law – just as energetically as the police in Chicago and New York had seventy-five years before, but not nearly as successfully. And yes, I often had a Chinese meal in Khartoum. Perhaps it's the Sudanese style of preparation but Chinese food always went better with a couple of pots of tea.

In the Nuba Mountains we'd had a more relaxed environment than living in Khartoum and in Kadugli we'd even had our own club bar where we could buy a beer, imported under diplomatic rules, but it was a different matter in the capital. The British Embassy, like most diplomatic missions, had a very friendly and hospitable staff bar where outsiders, if on an approved list of invitees, were allowed to come in for a couple of hours on a Friday evening but very strict standards of behaviour were demanded and rigidly enforced.

*

Diplomatic premises were, of course, exempt from the usual considerations regarding alcohol and most had some kind of entertainment facility. In the British Embassy this was called the 'Pickwick Club' where staff could bring expat guests to enjoy a relaxed evening atmosphere and some serious networking. On a Friday evening, over a completely legal beer in the Pickwick Club, I met a visiting consultant and the conversation turned to what I might do when my time with the UN was up. I'd originally planned on two years in Sudan and had been there for four so it was time to start looking to move on and he suggested I contact the British Red Cross Society. This conversation took place in about January. By February I had been sent the longest application form I'd ever seen and after taking days to fill it out it all seemed to fall into a black hole. In the summer of 2006 my contract ended and I left Sudan for the last time but shortly after getting home I had a meeting at the BRCS HQ in London and then I was asked to visit Geneva to meet the International Committee of the Red Cross.

I had one further trip to Africa but that comes later.

XIII

From 1859 Onwards

You might recall that in the Foreword I mentioned that this memoire began as an open letter to my grandchildren to tell them things I am unlikely to be around to talk about with them when they are old enough to understand. Some historical detail has been included to add background and colour and I have tried throughout to maintain a sense of the ridiculous even when it included me. But, in this chapter, something that you may notice is a change in style in that what I thought of as humorous incidents involving colleagues, and others, are lacking. This does not mean that such things did not happen, because they did on a regular basis. Elsewhere, in other contexts, I have included stories and events to show that even when dealing with extreme violence, suicide or working in active war zones, maintaining a sense of humanity is of overriding importance.

However, while I am grateful for the assistance given by both the British Red Cross Society (BRCS) and the International Committee of the Red Cross (ICRC), which has resulted in greater technical accuracy, there has, unfortunately, been some compression of timelines in order to preserve confidentiality, protect organisational, personal and national reputations and to observe 'diplomatic' protocols. BRCS and ICRC reviewers several times took issue with the 'tone' expressed, even calling it 'flippant' on a couple of occasions. In order to avoid any suggestion that I hold the Red Cross and Red Crescent Movement, usually simplified to just the 'Movement', in any but the highest regard, therefore, I have removed all references about which comments have been raised and, acknowledging the impossibility of obtaining 'consent' from people I met long ago in distant places, I have deleted incidents involving the Movement which might be thought irrelevant or trivial. Where I have expressed matters of personal opinion, I hope I have stayed within permissible bounds but I have included some illustrations to show what real life can be like. Even in stressful circumstances people are fundamentally the same everywhere.

2006

Describing what happened during the five years after leaving Sudan has been a difficult process. The Red Cross is able to function because it observes strict neutrality, impartiality and extremely high levels of confidentiality especially in its dealings with governments and others. Not only does this allow those with whom it engages on a daily basis to be open and, sometimes, honest about the situation 'on the ground' but provides a degree of safety and security for staff members, many of whom are nationals of the countries concerned and who might otherwise be exposed to personal risk.

You may also recall that earlier I acknowledged the help of Master Shakespeare in providing aliases for some of the people I've met during my wanderings, except the small number whose identities deserve to be known but, let me be quite clear, the only real persons identified in this last section before going home, are M. Henri Dunant – more of him later – Napoleon III, Victor Emmanuel II, Emperor Franz Joseph I, Joseph Stalin and Premier Nikita Khrushchev whose identities I see no reason to disguise. Every other character presented here is a composite of the various interesting, sometimes colourful, personalities I've had the pleasure of meeting. Similarly, while I am unable to be specific about most of the places or events in which I was involved, I hope you will be able to draw something of the flavour of the work if I simply mention that during five years I lived in, or travelled to, Armenia, Australia, Azerbaijan, Fiji, Georgia, Indonesia, Jordan, Kazakhstan, Kyrgyzstan, Malaysia, Pakistan, Papua New Guinea, Philippines, Russian Federation, Singapore, South Africa, Switzerland, Tajikistan, Thailand, Timor-Leste, Uganda, Ukraine, United Kingdom and Uzbekistan. (A good sense of the history of some of these regions can be gleaned from the works of Peter Hopkirk[6] which I strongly recommend. I didn't visit them alphabetically but I did go to many of them several times. A border control officer at one airport, on seeing my passport, still just two years old but bulging with visas, called his supervisor and left his booth to photocopy every page. He might have been impressed but the thirty people in the queue behind me were not.

1859

Battle of Solferino

The next couple of pages are really an overgrown footnote but I think it will help to mention a little of the historical context. Many people misunderstand the Red Cross largely because news media reporters, who are unable to think in more than three-word sound bites and banner headlines, can't be bothered to explain and probably don't fully understand it themselves. So, new readers start here please…

Despite what you read, hear or see on television, there is no such organisation as 'The International Red Cross'. In June 1859, a wealthy Swiss businessman by the name of Henri Dunant was passing through Italy and saw the aftermath of the Battle of Solferino between France and Austria. Strictly speaking, it was

---

6   *The Great Game. The Struggle for Empire in Central Asia*, Peter Hopkirk (1992), and several other titles by the same author.

between the Austrian Empire and the Second French Empire but the army of the Kingdom of Sardinia had been accorded the privilege of fighting, and in many cases dying, on the French side. Unlike most 'gentlemen' of the time who might visit a battle to watch the carnage as a sort of gladiatorial spectator sport from a safe vantage point, Dunant was moved by the sheer brutality of it and in particular that no special provisions had been made to care for the injured and dead. Napoleon III and Victor Emmanuel II had together fielded an army of 131,500 against 130,200 Austrians under Emperor Franz Joseph I. The French and Sardinian victors lost 5,400 dead and 12,100 wounded while the Austrians suffered casualties of 11,700 dead and 10,700 wounded.

Dunant stayed to organise assistance at the scene and later wrote *A Memory of Solferino*[7] in which he suggested the formation, in all countries, of voluntary relief societies for the prevention and alleviation of the suffering of wounded soldiers in wartime and the protection of medical personnel on the battlefield. He also proposed an international agreement in relation to the treatment of the wounded in conflict. The creation of the International Committee of the Red Cross (ICRC) in Geneva, as an independent, neutral and impartial humanitarian organisation, and the formation of National Red Cross Societies in each member state, came about as a result. The international agreements, to which he looked forward, we know now as the Geneva Conventions.[8]

Contrary to popular belief, the Red Cross emblem was not chosen as a Christian symbol but in recognition of the Swiss contribution by reversing the colours of the national flag of Switzerland of a white cross on a red ground.

The Geneva Conventions can only be signed by state parties and

---

7   Widely available through National Red Cross Societies and the ICRC; also in pdf format online.

8   The most recent iterations of what are usually referred to collectively as the 'Geneva Conventions' (GC) of 1949 concern protection of the wounded and medical personnel on land (GC I), at sea (GC II), the protection of prisoners of war (GC III) and of civilians (GC IV).

remain among the few international instruments accepted by every state body in the world. The ICRC is a fiercely independent, private Swiss organisation and not a department of the United Nations, part of the Swiss Government or an NGO. It is funded from a variety of sources including private donations and National Red Cross and Red Crescent societies. The largest donors are national governments, some of which are more generous than others and, certainly, without aid from countries such as Australia, Canada, Switzerland, UK and USA the ICRC would be in very grave financial difficulty. The list is alphabetical but neither exclusive nor prioritised and I apologise to those deserving and generous countries I have omitted.

Only one 'National Society', either of the Red Cross or Red Crescent, and approved by the ICRC in Geneva, can be established in each state. The use of a red crescent moon first appeared during the Russo-Turkish War (1876 to 1878) but was not formally adopted until the Geneva Conventions were revised in 1929. The 'National Society', as an auxiliary organisation, uses the chosen emblem of the medical services of the country's armed forces – whether the original Red Cross emblem or the later Red Crescent symbol – but cannot use both.

The four Geneva Conventions were last revised in 1949 but more recent evolution of the way in which modern international and internal conflicts take place was acknowledged by two further Additional Protocols which were added in 1977. In 2006, a third Additional Protocol authorised the use of a new emblem known as the Red Crystal, a red square set at forty-five degrees against a white ground and untainted by any religious or cultural significance. Other emblems have included the 'Red Lion and Sun' which had the same protected status under international law. The Geneva Conventions and Additional Protocols form the basis of what is collectively called International Humanitarian Law (IHL) often referred to, mainly by soldiers, as 'The Law of Armed Conflict' (LoAC) or the 'Laws of War' (LoW), terms which actually predate IHL. None of these expressions, however, should be confused with

International Human Rights Law (IHRL) which is a distinct and separate body of law.

Responsibility for actually delivering assistance falls to the National Red Cross or Red Crescent Society of the country in which the need arises but in just about all examples of modern conflict, demand far exceeds the available resources of any single national society. In cases of armed conflict, coordination becomes the responsibility of the ICRC. In cases of natural disaster, the International Federation of Red Cross and Red Crescent Societies (IFRC) will coordinate and manage assistance from other societies but in either case the national society of the country concerned is, at least nominally, in the lead. Thus, the broad division is that the ICRC looks after conflict while the IFRC deals in natural disaster. I personally never worked under anything but an ICRC flag. The Red Cross and Red Crescent Movement, is an overarching name covering all parts of the 'family' but always keep in mind that when you hear or read of 'The International Red Cross' the writer probably didn't understand.

Finally, a word about the Red Cross/Crescent/Crystal emblems. By far the most important thing about them is that they are protected symbols by law and must not be misused, which explains why you will see lots of green crosses in commercial logos. Other than national societies themselves, IFRC and ICRC, only military medical vehicles, ships and aircraft, facilities or personnel can use these emblems. It is a war crime to target any vehicle or premises under the protection of a 'Red Cross' flag as much as it is to carry or conceal operational soldiers or weapons in a Red Cross protected ambulance, station soldiers in a hospital or disguise them as medical personnel. Prohibitions apply even in peacetime although some countries observe these conditions more stringently than others and use of a conspicuous red cross in the markings of ordinary ambulances, pharmacies or clinics is not uncommon internationally; I can even think of one example of a clock repair workshop in the UK which used a red cross to advertise its services.

2006

Training, Training and More Training

Now well into the autumn of 2006 I found myself caught up in a round of medical checks and yet more form filling. (If ever medals are given for form filling, I can expect distinctions from the FCO, OSCE, UN, BRCS and ICRC. I'm an expert.) I'd already met the ICRC and while I was to be employed by the British Red Cross Society I was immediately seconded to Geneva. As I waited for a formal offer there was an induction course, this time just outside London, where the British Red Cross actually provided a couple of hours of first-aid training.

The movement places great emphasis on training and puts significant resources into preparing international delegates and national staff for the jobs they will do including sending them to distant places to meet colleagues from countries around the globe. After being despatched from London my first stop was in Geneva where a short induction course for newly appointed delegates in the 'FAS' department was held. The ICRC thinks of itself primarily as the education arm of the movement in relation to compliance with the Geneva Conventions in armed conflict by combatants and governments through a process of training, dissemination of material and 'soft' diplomacy. Internally, the *Forces Armées et de Sécurité* (FAS) department at ICRC HQ in Geneva was the lead branch and would be my new home base but police were an uncomfortable fit in the FAS department and still regarded as something of a curiosity as the Geneva Conventions don't really have much to say about them. I'd been out of the policing business myself long enough now to talk about 'them' and not 'us' and was part of a relatively new group of 'PSF' (*Police and Security Forces*) delegates.

I spent a few days in Geneva learning not about the role itself but the way in which the ICRC wanted it done: very detailed and precise. The real job, however, was elsewhere in a region where an active civil war was still being fought and in many ways was similar to what I had been doing before in the Balkans and Africa, namely liaising with police and government authorities at ministerial and headquarters level but now, rarely going to the field.

However, the training wasn't yet even halfway over. Before I'd arrived in Geneva, I had been told that I would be sent on to a cold and snowy winter so I'd packed accordingly but after Geneva came an ICRC course at Petra, in Jordan, for ICRC staff from a number of different delegations. There's no such thing as bad weather, there's only inappropriate clothing and I was now in the desert in Jordan dressed for the Arctic. Petra is an incredible place whatever the season; the red stone is layered in vivid colours and was once a Roman settlement where whole buildings had been chiselled out of the living rock. Probably the most famous of these is the columned facade of the 'Monastery' at the head of the narrow gorge between high cliffs leading into the site and of which film makers have made good use. Over the centuries other large temples and houses have been carved from the solid stone, a deeply tiered theatre and an altar on which the blood channels were so red they looked as if they might still have been in use. The view from the top swept across the city to the horizon and it was chilling to think of the number of people for whom this had been their last view of anything at all.

After a couple of weeks in Petra it was back to Amman overnight before travelling on, at last, to my assignment. Everyone on the course had been given an onward air ticket leaving at different times, so as the evening wore on our number steadily thinned out. I was due to leave at about 2am the next morning and late in the evening about half a dozen of us remained in a restaurant in the city having dinner. Smoking in restaurants was still the norm but here it was difficult to see the ceiling so a lady in our group asked a waiter if there was a smoke-free area. Deeply shocked, he immediately summoned the manager who realised that although the complainer was a woman, she was still a foreigner, so concessions would have to be made. "Yes, of course. I will create a no-smoking area especially for you," and he

took the ashtray away from our table. It was now a no-smoking zone
– problem solved.

*

I eventually flew from Amman, via Frankfurt to Pulkovo Airport in
St Petersburg, where I arrived on 23rd November shortly after 11pm;
I had left Amman in plus twenty degrees and arrived in minus ten
degrees and when I stepped off the flight I was as cold as I'd ever
been in my life but at least I was now dressed appropriately. The
ICRC delegation in Moscow had found me a slot on a one-month
'total immersion' language course in St Petersburg where my choice
of clothing would now prove to be worth the extra weight. A taxi
driver at the airport had a sign showing he was waiting for 'Mr D.
Amman' and took me directly to the home of my host for the next
month, incorporating a bit of practice for the high-speed ice-driving
team on the way. If you were Mr D. Amman whose pre-booked taxi
was hijacked by another passenger, I sincerely apologise. This was the
first of what would become many visits to Russia which, like Africa,
is unique and everyone should try to experience it at least once.

During the Second World War, always known in Russia as the
'Great Patriotic War', St. Petersburg, then called Leningrad, had been
almost razed by German forces during a siege which lasted from 1941
to 1944. Almost three and a half million military personnel had been
killed, injured, captured or simply listed as missing. A further million
civilians, probably about thirty per cent of the population, also died
many of them starving or freezing to death. Most wooden buildings,
many in the classical Russian style, were destroyed and burned as
firewood. Even today some of the older apartments which survived
still show the scorch marks on otherwise immaculate parquet floors.
Unsurprisingly the siege is, even now, a very sensitive subject for
Russians. Only the central area of the city had survived but this,
fortunately, included many of the iconic places such as the Hermitage
Museum, Nevski Prospekt and St Isaac's Cathedral. After the death

of Joseph Stalin in 1953, Premier Nikita Khrushchev commissioned an architect, whose previous career had seemingly been designing shoe boxes, to build hundreds of identical, characterless, concrete blocks which provided just about adequate accommodation.

For the purpose of my language training in St Petersburg I had been given a choice of either staying in a hotel or at a private house as a lodger. Children are always excellent language teachers so I'd opted for a private house but it did not turn out to be quite what I expected. Almost no one in a Russian city actually lives in a house but usually in an apartment and for the next month I was to be a guest of an elderly widow who had at least two other jobs apart from taking in lodgers from the language school. She had no children which was as well because her apartment was tiny and in which I think I probably had the largest room. When my taxi driver dropped me in the street outside the block she was already waiting and took me up to her flat on the seventh floor. She had very limited English, and asked me if I liked borsch. (No, this isn't a trick. 'Borsch' is a Ukrainian dish but I was not in Ukraine.) I did, and still do, like borsch. She gave me a set of keys, showed me where I would find cheese, eggs, milk, bread and coffee for breakfast and put out some excellent borsch. I think I saw her again about twice in the following month.

Learning a new language becomes more difficult with age especially an ancient language which is more like a form of very hi-tech verbal encryption designed to prevent foreigners understanding what people around them are talking about. The alphabet was actually quite simple and was more or less the Greek alphabet with thirty-three letters, thirty-one of which each make one sound while the other two modify the sound of the previous letter; there were no double letters. But then came the complications of having six cases and three genders, all of which might change the words, spellings and grammar and, oh, have you allowed for plural and singular forms? I would have to live in this for the next month. On my first day at the school my passport was taken away for a special long-term visa and issue of a diplomatic ID card so, until it came back, I couldn't escape even if I'd wanted to.

*

It was now December. The sun barely crept over the horizon before 10am and was gone before 4pm, so my journey to and from the school every day was always in the bitterly cold darkness of a northern Russian winter. Everyone remarked on the strange absence of snow as there had only been a couple of very light falls so far but it was unusually mild, by local standards, with temperatures hovering around minus four or minus five degrees, so at the weekends I was able to be a tourist for a few hours before getting back to the flat to do my homework. Exploring St Petersburg on foot was interesting but outside the centre there was little to see except grey concrete.

Travelling on the bus from my apartment to the centre of the city was an introduction to local culture compressed into ten minutes which you won't even find in a *Lonely Planet* guide. The route was served by both city and privately owned vehicles on which the fare was standard but the buses themselves were a bit of an eclectic fleet. My favourite was a gas-powered thirty-five-seater which still carried its original Chinese number plates as well as the local ones. It was privately owned but the driver had a licence to ply the route and at weekends would often have his twelve-year-old son walking the aisle collecting fares. It was all very relaxed. I usually had to stand and watch as the driver passed his son change for tickets over his shoulder, took a call on his mobile phone or a bite of his sandwich. Sometimes he'd even take both hands off the wheel to take a swig at his drink or use the phone but was quite good at steering with his knees for a moment or two.

By far the best way to get round the city was on the Metro and, although the St Petersburg system was not as extensive as in some other countries, it was much more elaborately decorated with fabulous use of marble and bronze, mosaics and statues. One location was not so much a Metro station with statues but more a subterranean Roman temple with trains. The whole system was almost surgically clean – you simply did not drop litter or daub graffiti on the Metro and smoking had never been allowed. Trains ran every few minutes and on time. (TFL, please note.) The main point of confusion for visitors was that where lines crossed, stations on each line would have a different name. Imagine Liverpool Street on the Central Line being known as Old Broad Street on the Circle Line, but you got used to it in time. Walking around the city also got me used to the local habit of keeping buildings stiflingly warm inside and I started to go to cafés that were not on the usual tourist agenda but sold something other than borsch. Outside the Hermitage Museum I walked around with a hot chocolate as thick as soup, and made with more brandy than you'd want if you had to drive, watching teams of students working on their ten-foot-high ice sculptures with chisels and blow-lamps. The finished sculptures were still there when I left three weeks later.

Oh, and I learned a bit of the language, too.

2007

I returned to Geneva for yet another training and briefing session in January 2007. The weather in both places was awful and Heathrow had been just about closed down by fog. Geneva is a great city if you happen to be a billionaire and I walked around the central area, across to the French side of the lake, out to the Jet d'Eau Fountain (extremely noisy and get the wind direction right or you'll get soaked) but, overall, unless you are skiing in winter or boating in summer, it's pretty dull especially at weekends. The shops in the city centre, if they're open at all, have mostly closed by midday on Saturday and it's a ghost town on Sunday. One evening I idly totted up the value of the cars outside Le Richemond Hotel and got lost in the zeros. How often will you see a Maserati, a Ferrari and a Bugatti Veyron in a line with a new Bentley Continental GTC double parked beside them?

Better to get back to the hotel and carry on reading the Geneva Conventions and detailed handouts on ICRC financial planning – but then I've always known how to have a good time.

*

At the beginning of February I was, at last, given the air ticket which would take me on to my assignment in Moscow. A colleague from the delegation met me on arrival and his genuinely warm greeting allowed me to relax and look forward positively to getting down to work. After another high-speed ride through grey slush to the city centre I was deposited at the apartment which had been allocated for me in a block, I later found out, owned by the Ministry of Foreign Affairs. In the area behind I could see the tops of slides and swings for children coming through the snow but what I thought were landscaped gardens were the humps of cars hibernating under the snow since November which would stay there until it was safe for them to emerge in March.

But getting down to work would have to wait for a few weeks yet. First there was a FAS conference to attend back in Geneva, same hotel (same room!) but at least this time I had the company of a colleague who, I think, was actually just a little impressed with how well I knew my way around the city being neither an Olympic skier nor a billionaire. Later still my frequent-flyer account would be further topped up by a trip across two continents to observe at a series of seminars for senior police officers but at least it was in a country I'd not been to before. Probably the most memorable part of that trip was coming back to my hotel room one night to find the largest, hairiest black spider I've ever seen sitting in the middle of my bed. I am not especially arachnophobic – spiders are entitled to their place in Creation just as much as cute and fluffy little kittens – but not in my bed. I was very pleased that I would be flying out the next day.

Between April and August, although I was able to make some limited and tentative contacts within the law enforcement agencies in the countries within my remit, wheels were turning elsewhere and at the end of the summer I was informed that I would shortly be heading for a new assignment. The transfer required a return visit to Geneva to be debriefed after which the BRCS wanted to see me in London for more debriefing and then briefing about my next assignment. I also had to get medical clearance, which was completed in London, before flying out, yet again, to Geneva for a week of preparation with a profound feeling of déjà vu.

*

In the next four plus years I went to countries that, before the days of cheap air travel, many people might have remembered from their primary school geography classes but probably wouldn't have been able to find on a map. They were different in ways too numerous to list but shared much more in common. In all cases there was an ongoing conflict, either internal or external, or the burgeoning threat of one, or else problems were being addressed arising from post-conflict reconstruction and development. In some, but not all, the National Red Cross Society, or National Red Crescent Society, was actively present in the field assisting with practical distribution of aid while the ICRC sought to develop a closer relationship with military forces, police and security services as well as other agencies working towards common goals. In most I found I was welcomed at government level. Most governments had come through their periods of conflict and were stabilising as their relationships with their own regional partners became more secure. Others were much more fragile and I arrived in one capital just as the government collapsed. Elsewhere I met child soldiers just like those I'd seen years before in Sudan.

I concentrated on organising seminars for senior-level police officers in which we examined the concepts of the 'Rule of Law' and 'Community Policing', which are almost universally misunderstood as meaning law enforcement by formal police forces. International standards and norms in law enforcement, use of force, including lethal force, use of weapons, public order, ethical standards and the definition of torture were included and often generated lively debate. But, sadly, that's about all I can say about my work during the four-year period before I returned home. The ICRC is still present in all of the places I worked and relationships with host governments can be sensitive. I have been privileged to be able to contribute, at various times and places, to processes that have ended wars and helped developing countries emerging from conflict but, although I might loftily try to claim that working towards World Peace has been my goal, it would be more truthful to say that my personal incentive has always been simply to travel to meet people and try to experience something of their lives.

For Example...

During a brief visit to Timor-Leste I stayed on the beach at the Hotel California, where you really can check in any time you like. The hotel was as cheap as you would expect of any guest house built almost entirely from palm-wood logs and woven screens but if I ever go there again I would not consider staying anywhere else. I only had one meal at the hotel; there was no menu, the barman asked what I wanted, then he told the cook I said I'd like crab so the cook went down to the water and caught one for me. They won't do that for you in a Harvester or a Wetherspoon's. The only two other guests were a retired Australian dentist and a Polish motor mechanic of about the same age. These two gentlemen had been born in the same town in Poland in the 1950s where they'd gone to school together. One had emigrated with his parents to Australia but they had kept in touch over the next fifty-odd years and they always wanted to get together again. Some years before, the Australian had gone to Poland and he and his old school chum, both now retired widowers, had bought a pair of huge BMW motorcycles and decided to ride around the world. It had taken them three years to get as far as Timor-Leste on the leg of their journey which would take them, eventually, to Darwin then Brisbane. When I met them, they'd been staying at Hotel California for three months – it's possible that they're still there.

Walking along the beach one night I met an old man sitting under a tree cooking fish over an open fire. Up in the branches of the tree were three or four rusty and corroded cannon barrels, obviously recovered from the sea. The Portuguese had lost many ships over four hundred years but why anyone should (a) drag these ashore and (b) put them in the tree was a mystery. The old beach cook offered to tell me for $5. It seemed his papa had been a pearl diver and had found the wreck of an old Portuguese warship in an area where he wanted to dive for oysters. To give himself room he'd pulled the barrels ashore and just dumped them on the beach where a tree had grown under them and pushed them up to where they were now about 10 feet off the ground. The story took twenty minutes and was good value for money.

*

Now, imagine that you are a villager in Indonesia, or Timor-Leste or Borneo. You work all day in the plantation, in the sun, tending the coffee plants, especially trying to stop animals from eating the precious cherries containing the coffee beans on which your livelihood depends. One day you notice that civet cats, weasel-like nuisances that eat the coffee cherries, have left piles of their droppings under the plants consisting mainly of partially digested coffee beans. Later that night, when your fellow plantation workers ask why you've brought back a bag of rat droppings you just smile and say you're going to roast them, grind them up and drink the result. They think you've been in the sun maybe a bit too long and no one in the village wants to join you for coffee that night. Very soon you are extremely rich and your fellow workers are still hoeing the weeds between the rows of bushes.

'Civet' coffee is produced throughout South East Asia which has resulted in Asian 'palm civets' increasingly being taken from the wild and sold on to coffee producers. The jury is still out on what actually contributes to the flavour; whether it's fussiness in the selection of the cherries by the civets or the effect of partial digestion on the way through the animal's digestive tract. Whatever, the result is a coffee which retails for up to £500 per kilogram. I had some in Manila. What did it taste like? It tasted like coffee. But if in future when you make someone a cup of coffee, they grimace and say it tastes like 'cat s***' they are actually paying you a great compliment. You can't get it in Tesco yet but I'm not sure about Waitrose.

*

In 2009 the ICRC decided that my talents were required in Central Asia and I was reassigned to the delegation based in Tashkent. As a socialist state and former member of the USSR, Uzbekistan could not have a patron saint but if they had it would have been Amir Timur, better known in the West as 'Tamerlane'. The name actually comes from the Persian meaning 'Timur the Lame' and was regarded as being highly insulting. It was unwise in the extreme to use it to modern-day Uzbeks who didn't like to be reminded of his reputed deformity and reactions might range from getting your coffee spilled in your lap to being very thoroughly searched at customs. Timur was born in Uzbekistan in 1336 and died at the grand age of sixty-eight in 1405 in what is now Kazakhstan. Like other great historical leaders, such as King Henry VIII and Tsar Peter the Great, long after verification was possible, he was credited with having found time to acquire an intimate and expert knowledge of the arts and sciences, have frequent interaction with the great intellects of his day, invent a variant of chess played on a board of 10x10 squares, all while riding across what is now Central Asia to wage wars of conquest in which he never lost a battle. Much of the wealth he plundered from elsewhere was used to make his capital at Samarkand, one of the most fabulous cities of the time. His reputation was one of extreme cruelty and he was reputed to have built a tower of the still living prisoners of his conquests, bound together with clay, which stood as a mark of his power for a century. Pictures and statues show the thin Asiatic features of a snarling man who probably wasn't a good loser at 10x10 Superchess. He was almost invariably depicted mounted, armoured and ready for battle. In the centre of Tashkent was a very restfully laid out park in which all the paths led to the high stone plinth in the middle from where Amir Timur glowered down from his horse.

*

Tashkent was the departure point from which I would eventually return to the UK. The most famous market in Tashkent was the Alayski Bazar – spellings vary – where it was possible to buy anything that was in season and always very fresh. The spice hall was lined with ladies selling finely ground powders in amazing primary colours and seeds and spices piled high in huge flat baskets. A kind of lemon was sold there that was so sweet it could be eaten like an orange. One section of the market was exclusively for leather workers and furriers next to the alley for kitchen equipment. There was also a pretty extensive range of swords, daggers, flick-knives, axes and other toys which every man seemed to carry although I cannot recall a single instance of them being used in anger in all the time I was there.

*

Florists in Tashkent did good business all year because flowers were popular, plentiful and cheap. Except on one day of the year when, despite there being no shortage, prices doubled or even trebled. Prior to starting work abroad I wasn't really aware of 8th March as being International Women's Day. Its origins go back to 1909 and American socialism but in 1917 the new infant Soviet Russia – the USSR did not come into existence until December 1922 – declared 8th March a national holiday and it is still marked that way in modern Russia and most of the former Soviet member states today. It was not acknowledged by the UN until 1977 and it's only in recent years that people in the West have become aware of it.

But recognition of Women's Day was big business. It was an unspoken rule that every man would buy flowers for each lady of his acquaintance; 'unspoken' in the sense that the ladies would speak of little else if any man was silly enough to forget. This rule applied even more so at home where something more meaningful, i.e. more expensive, was expected.

The Chevrolet Matiz was one of the most popular cars on the roads in Tashkent. They were small and cheap but not really very practical for Uzbek men who tended towards generosity of stature. In the late afternoon on Monday 8th March 2010, I can be sure of the date, I was driving a large, heavy Toyota 4x4 with mirrors on very solid extended arms about four feet above ground level and stopped to turn left at traffic lights. I noticed a little Matiz coming towards me driven by a man holding a bunch of flowers so large it would not fit inside the car so he held it outside with his left hand while he steered with his right (we're driving on the right, remember). He had right of way so I intended just to let him pass and then turn left behind him. Maybe it was because of the splendid bouquet but he took a line through the junction so close to me that the flowers whipped under the mirror arm at about 30 mph and were neatly scythed off. I was left sitting in the middle of the junction enveloped by the sort of flower petal storm you'd usually expect in artfully staged wedding photographs but could see the Matiz in the mirror as it carried on up the road with an arm out of the window holding a bunch of decapitated stalks. If the driver had any sense he was going back to find a florist before they closed for the day.

*

I don't know whether Winston Churchill had any of the countries where I've worked, except the UK, specifically in mind when he said, "Democracy is the worst form of government, except for all the others," but it has applied in just about every case and made navigating the sensitivities of all aspects of life extremely interesting from dealing with government to getting in a taxi when tribal loyalty, political party membership and pressures of endemic corruption had to be taken into account. I am not speaking here, of course, about places I've visited and people I've encountered in my experience in the movement but include the Balkans, Africa and even the UK. I've already mentioned that I'd learned more about African tribal loyalty in half an hour from a New York taxi driver than I did from living in Africa for four years.

Going Home

On leaving an assignment in most organisations it's usual to put together some kind of handover or 'End of Mission Report' for the information of the commander at HQ, the local head of department or office but, most importantly, whoever will take on the job next. A face-to-face handover would usually be best but, unfortunately, I rarely received one nor was I often able to meet my successor.

In October 2011 my contract expired and I had to consider what I was going to do next and where I would go. I hadn't really lived in the UK since leaving in 1999 to go to Kosovo and, despite having been back on leave many times, returning now to resume residence was a chilling prospect with lots of practical problems. When did the cost of a newspaper go over £1? Why was everyone walking around staring at a little glass screen? – I'd had a mobile phone for years but I only used mine to speak to people. I was lucky that even though I was a product of London I had always felt more comfortable out of town and after so many years away from Britain it seemed much more natural to settle in a rural area and try to fit in. The FCO and DfID were prepared to talk to me and even regarded a few years' experience with the UN, BRCS and ICRC a positive advantage, so after I'd managed to convince a vetting officer that I wasn't a risk to national security, eventually I was able to work with HMG again as a consultant.

A friend had a poster on his office wall which read,

If you're not part of the solution, you're part of the problem – but either way there's still good money to be made in consultancy.

Glossary of Terms and Acronyms

AK	Avtomat Kalashnikova (Designation of AK assault rifle series designed by Mikhail Kalashnikov including the ubiquitous AK47)
aka	Also known as
AoR	Area of Responsibility
APM	Anti-Personnel Mine(s)
BBC	British Broadcasting Corporation
BBQ	Barbeque
BEM	British Empire Medal
BiH	Bosna i Hercegovina (Bosnia and Herzegovina)
BRCS	British Red Cross Society
BSc	Batchelor of Science
CD	Corps Diplomatique (plate displayed on vehicles with protected status under the Vienna Convention 1963)
CDG	Paris (Charles de Gaulle airport code)
CID	Criminal Investigation Department
CIS	Commonwealth of Independent States (economic and political successor to USSR) (Don't confuse 'CIS' with 'cis'. They are very different and could get you in a lot of trouble in Moscow.)
CIS	Communication and Information Systems (UK Armed Forces)
CO	Commissioner's Office (Scotland Yard. Headquarters office of the Metropolitan Police)
CoLP	City of London Police

CW	Chemical Weapons
DAC	Deputy Assistant Commissioner
DC	Detective Constable
DCI	Detective Chief Inspector
DDA	Detective Duty Allowance
DfID	Department for International Development (UK) (see also USAID)
DI	Detective Inspector
DIY	Do-It-Yourself
DM	Doctorate of Medicine
DNA	Deoxyribonucleic acid
DPKO	(United Nations) Department of Peace Keeping Operations
DPU	Depleted Uranium (ammunition)
DS	Detective Sergeant
ESCO	(United Nations) Educational, Scientific and Cultural Organization
EU	European Union
FAS	Forces Armées et de Sécurité (ICRC Department for Military and Security Forces. See also PSF)
FCO	(UK) Foreign & Commonwealth Office (equivalent to Ministry of Foreign Affairs)
FRCP	Fellow of the Royal College of Physicians
FYROM	Former Yugoslav Republic of Macedonia
GC	Geneva Convention(s)
GC	George Cross
GOD	Good Order & Discipline
GoS	Government of Sudan
GoSS	Government of South Sudan
GPS	Global Positioning System
GVA	Geneva (Geneva airport code)
HAZMAT	Hazardous Material
HCHR	(United Nations) High Commission for Human Rights
HCR	(United Nations) High Commission for Refugees
HDZ	Hrvatska Demokratska Zajednic (Croatian Democratic

	Union, literally Croatian Democratic Community)
HFO	Head of Field Office
HMG	Her Majesty's Government
HMMWV	High Mobility Multi-purpose Wheeled Vehicle (also known as a Humvee or Hummer)
HO	(UK) Home Office (equivalent to Ministry of Interior)
HoD	Head of Delegation
HoM	Head of Mission
HQ	Headquarters
ICJ	International Court of Justice
ICRC	International Committee of the Red Cross
ID	Identity (card or document)
IDP	Internally Displaced Persons
IF	Irregular Forces
IFRC	International Federation of Red Cross and Red Crescent Societies
IGO	Inter-Governmental Organisation
IHL	International Humanitarian Law
IHRL	International Human Rights Law
IT	Ill Treatment (of civilian populations or prisoners)
IT	Information Technology
IT	Interior Troops
IT	International Terrorist / International Terrorism
JFK	John Fitzgerald Kennedy International Airport New York
JMC	Joint Military Commission (Sudan cease-fire monitoring team)
JMM	Joint Monitoring Mission (Sudan)
JP	Justice of the Peace/Magistrate
KLA	Kosovo Liberation Army (see also UCK)
KVM	Kosovo Verification Mission (see also OSCE)
LE	Little Engine (Velocette motor cycle designation)
LoAC	Law of Armed Conflict
LoW	Laws of War

Met	Metropolitan Police Service
Mi-8	(МИ-8) Russian built helicopter
MoD	Ministry of Defence
MPS	Metropolitan Police Service
MSF	Médecins Sans Frontières
MVD	Russian Ministry of Internal Affairs (Ministerstvo Vnutrennikh Del, *Министерство внутренних дел*). General term for 'Police'.
NATO	North Atlantic Treaty Organisation
NGO	Non-Governmental Organisation
ODHIR	Office for Democratic Institutions and Human Rights (see also OSCE)
OSCE	Organisation for Security and Cooperation in Europe (see also KVM and ODHIR)
PA	Personal Assistant
PA	Personnel Assistant
PA	Police (or Policing) Advisor
PA	Policy Adviser
PA	Political Adviser
PA	Press Adviser
PC	Police Constable
PNP	Philippines National Police
POLACC	Police Accident (Met – traffic accident involving a police vehicle)
POW	Prisoners of War
PS	Police Sergeant
PSF	Police and Security Forces (Section within the ICRC FAS Dept.)
RAF	Royal Air Force
RF	Russian Federation
RIP	Rest in Peace
RPG	Rocket Propelled Grenade
RSM	Regimental Sergeant Major
Sci-Fi	Science Fiction

SO	Specialist Operations
SPLA	Sudan People's Liberation Army
SPLM	Sudan People's Liberation Movement
SRSG	Special Representative of the Secretary General
SW	South West
TA	Threat Assessment
TARDIS	Time And Relative Dimension In Space
TDC	Temporary Detective Constable
TFL	Transport for London
TV	Television
UÇK	Albanian acronym of the Kosovo Liberation Army or UÇK for Ushtria Çlirimtare e Kosovës (see also KLA)
UK	United Kingdom
UN	United Nations
UNDPKO	United Nations Department of Peace Keeping Operations
UNESCO	United Nations Educational, Scientific and Cultural Organization
UNHCHR	United Nations High Commission for Human Rights
UNHCR	United Nations High Commission for Refugees
UNMIS	United Nations Mission in Sudan
UNP	United Nations Personnel
UNSCR	United Nations Security Council Resolution
US(A)	United States (of America)
USAID	United States Agency for International Development (see also DfID)
USD	Currency – United States Dollars ($) (the common currency of the universe)
USSR	Union of Soviet Socialist Republic (see also CIS)
UWSU	Underwater Search Unit
UXO	Unexploded Ordnance
VW	Volkswagen
WHO	(United Nations) World Health Organisation
WWII	World War II